Early Modern & Epistles

A Family Study Handbook

*Combining all your students (grades 1–12)
for History, Geography, and Bible*

by
Sonya Shafer

Early Modern and Epistles: A Family Study Handbook
© 2011, Sonya Shafer

Cover Design: Ruth Shafer

ISBN 978-1-61634-114-5

Published by
Simply Charlotte Mason, LLC
P.O. Box 892
Grayson, Georgia 30017-0892

SimplyCharlotteMason.com

Contents

Introduction

I love to teach Bible history along with world events, and the first three handbooks in this series focus on Bible history from Genesis through Acts. Some time is spent studying world events that happened during those years, but the emphasis is on Biblical history.

With the fourth handbook, the focus changes a little. We no longer have Biblical events to study, and world history picks up the pace. So with the fourth, fifth, and sixth books, we delve into learning about people who lived in the past since the time of the book of Acts, and we combine that study with timeless truths from the Epistles. This fifth book focuses on Early Modern history, about 1550 to 1850.

The lessons in this book will walk you through living books to read, Scripture passages to study, and optional hands-on activities to do. You'll also find narration ideas, teaching tips, exam questions, and Book of Centuries dates.

One of my main goals is to show you how you can teach the same historical time period to all of your children at the same time, no matter what grades they are in. I firmly believe in the advantages that a one-room schoolhouse approach can bring. You will save time in both planning and teaching, and your children will grow together in community as they learn together and help each other.

Please keep in mind that this study is just a collection of suggestions. I'm simply passing along these suggestions to, hopefully, save you some time and give you some ideas. You know your children much better than I do, so feel free to change, add, or omit as you see fit. Remember, I used the books that were available to me; they may not be available to you. Don't be afraid to substitute.

Most of all, encourage the older children to help the younger, and allow the younger to look over the shoulder of the older; and together, enjoy these family studies of History, Geography, and God's Word.

How to Use

Pace

The lessons are divided into three Terms. If you do five lessons each week, you should be able to cover a Term in about twelve weeks. Each week is divided into two days of World History, one day of Geography and Bible, and two days of American History. With this format you should be able to easily substitute your own country's history if you are not American. We have tried to save the final week of each Term for exams or to finish up any projects or assignments.

The chart below gives an overview of what is covered each Term. You will find more detailed charts, outlining work week by week, at the beginning of the Terms' lesson plans.

	American History (2 days/week)	Geography & Bible (1 day/week)	World History (2 days/week)
Term 1	Columbus through Colonial Times	South America & Ephesians; Philippians; Colossians; Philemon	Queen Elizabeth through Galileo
Term 2	French and Indian War through Causes of the Revolution	Australia & Hebrews	Dutch East India Company through Catherine the Great
Term 3	Revolution through the Alamo	Central America & 1, 2 Timothy; Titus	Napoleon through Garibaldi

Assignments

This book contains assignments and activities for every grade level so you can combine all your students into one family study. The "Family" instructions are for everyone to do together, then additional assignments are given for various grade levels to complete either independently or with the parent.

The hands-on activities are optional. Feel free to skip them, substitute different ones, or add more. You will find lots of helpful information and Internet links on the Links and Tips page for this book on our Web site at http://SimplyCharlotteMason.com/books/early-modern/links-tips

Note: Don't worry about days when you might skip the lesson for younger children but still do a lesson with the older children. Think of it as a day that the younger children can ruminate on what they have already learned. Charlotte encouraged reflecting, or ruminating, on what is read or heard: ". . . Reflection, the ruminating power which is so strongly developed in children and is somehow lost with much besides of the precious cargo they bring with them into the world. There is nothing sadder than the way we allow intellectual impressions to pass over the surface of our minds, without any effort to retain or assimilate" (Vol. 3, p. 120). "Children must be allowed to ruminate, must be left alone with their own thoughts" (Vol. 3, p. 162).

Resources Needed

A complete list of resources is given on pages 15–17 for all three Terms. Each Term's resources are listed in the lesson plans. Reminders are sprinkled throughout the lessons that will help you look ahead a week or so in order to give yourself enough time to locate the books you will need, especially if you are borrowing them as you go.

Map Drill

One part of most Geography lessons will be a map drill. Here's how we do map drill. Keep lessons short, no longer than ten or fifteen minutes. Once a week, give each child a blank map of the region you are studying and provide a detailed and labeled map of the same region. Instruct the child to label a few areas of the region, being careful to copy the names correctly from the detailed map. The next week, give the child another blank map of the same region and instruct her to label as many areas as she can remember. Once she has labeled all that she knows, display the detailed map and check for accuracy, then have her label a few more areas carefully. Continue this routine each week, and over the course of the year she will become quite familiar with the regions studied using this gentle method.

A Word about Charlotte Mason Methods Used in This Study

Living Books

Probably the most well known of Charlotte Mason's methods is her use of living books instead of dry, factual textbooks. Living books are usually written by one person who has a passion for the subject and writes in conversational or narrative style. The books pull you into the subject and involve your emotions, so it's easy to remember the events and facts. Living books make the subject "come alive." The books used in this study are living books. If you make a substitution, please do your best to select a living book.

Bible Readings

The Bible is the best living book! And Charlotte encouraged us to give our children plenty of direct contact with the Bible itself, not feed them just watered down retellings. So you will find throughout the lessons, the Scripture passages to read aloud directly from the Bible.

Narration

When you ask a child to narrate, you're asking him to tell back in his own words what he just saw, heard, or read. The narration can be oral or written or drawn— whatever. Because the child must think through the information and determine how to present it, mixed with his own opinion and impressions, this method of evaluation requires a much higher thinking level than mere fill-in-the-blank or answer-the-posed-question-with-a-fact methods. When requesting a child to narrate, word the question in an open, essay-type form, such as "Tell all you know about ___" or "Describe ___."

Oral Narration with Many Children: Usually it's good to start with the youngest child, then work your way up the ages asking if each has anything to add. However, if you use this approach every single time, the older ones might get complacent. ("No, nothing to add.") So you can mix things up a little by calling on any child at random to start the narration sometimes. Not knowing who will be selected to give the oral narration keeps everybody alert and listening. The key is to have one child start the narration and then have the others add to it, not repeat it. That mental exercise of remembering what was already mentioned and searching through your mind for something new to talk about is also a plus!

Written Narration: Older children can be expected to take the next step and write their narrations. If your older child is not used to doing narration, give him several weeks or months to get used to the idea and have practice narrating orally first. It's harder to keep your train of thought when you have to also think about the mechanics of writing, punctuating, capitalizing, and all such trappings, so make sure your child is adept and successful with organizing and expressing his thoughts orally before adding the writing aspect. Once he is an "old pro" at oral narrations, you can ease him into the written narrations by requiring just one a week or so to begin with. The lessons in this book will give suggestions for some written narrations. You can determine which of your students can handle those assignments.

Also keep in mind that you can do narration in many ways. Oral is the quickest and simplest. But if you would like to keep things fresh, you can have the children express what they learned in various ways. We have a list of narration ideas on the Web site that might help you: http://SimplyCharlotteMason.com/timesavers/narration/

Book of Centuries

A Book of Centuries is like a timeline in a notebook. As its name suggests, each two-page spread in the book is devoted to one hundred years—a century—of history. Each student creates his or her own book, recording historical events and names of importance, along with pictures, poems, quotes, and anything else that makes the book individual. You can also add written narrations, illustrations from the Internet, or titles of books you've read that are set in that time period. As they add more history to the book, they begin to make relations between people who lived in the same era.

Books of Centuries can be as simple or elaborate as you desire. If you want a simple one, download a free Book of Centuries template at SimplyCharlotteMason.com/timesavers/boc/

We recommend each student in grades 7–12 create his own Book of Centuries. If your students are not yet old enough to take on the responsibility of their own Books of Centuries, you could create one together as a family.

Watch for helpful dates in the timeline column throughout the lessons in this book. You don't have to add every event listed; feel free to pick and choose or add some of your own.

Resources Needed

American History
- *Stories of America, Volume 1*, by Charles Morris and Sonya Shafer
  Though written for the younger grades, this gentle introduction to American history will make a nice Family spine, contribute some additional biographies and information, and help tie together the different characters the older students will be reading about.

Grades 1–3
- *The Pilgrims of Plimoth* by Marcia Sewall
- *Samuel Eaton's Day: A Day in the Life of a Pilgrim Boy* by Kate Waters
- *Sarah Morton's Day: A Day in the Life of a Pilgrim Girl* by Kate Waters
- *Tapenum's Day: A Wampanoag Indian Boy in Pilgrim Times* by Kate Waters
- *The Courage of Sarah Noble* by Alice Dalgliesh
- *Toliver's Secret* by Esther Wood Brady
- *Benjamin Franklin* by Ingri and Edgar Parin D'Aulaire

Grades 4–6
- *The Landing of the Pilgrims* by James Daugherty
- *The Sign of the Beaver* by Elizabeth George Speare
- *A Young Patriot: The American Revolution as Experienced by One Boy* by Jim Murphy
- *Amos Fortune, Free Man* by Elizabeth Yates

Grades 7–9
- *Poor Richard* by James Daugherty
- *Carry On, Mr. Bowditch* by Jean Lee Latham
- *Early Thunder* by Jean Fritz OR *Johnny Tremain* by Esther Forbes
  Both books make for excellent reading and adventure in the pre-Revolutionary time period. They are both the same length and about the same reading level, so use whichever you have handy.
- *Lewis and Clark: The Journey of the Corps of Discovery* by Dayton Duncan and Ken Burns
  Note: A DVD set by the same name is also available. This Ken Burns production contains wonderful cinematography and really brings the Lewis and Clark expedition to life. Highly recommended if you have access to a copy and want to supplement the book.
- Book of Centuries (one for each student)

Grades 10–12
- *The Autobiography of Benjamin Franklin* by Benjamin Franklin
- *American Voices: A Collection of Documents, Speeches, Essays, Hymns, Poems, and Short Stories from American History* edited by Ray Notgrass
  This collection will be used over two years. Selections will be assigned throughout this handbook and in the Modern handbook that covers 1850 through present day.
- *The Boys of '76* by Charles Coffin
- *Lewis and Clark: The Journey of the Corps of Discovery* by Dayton Duncan and Ken Burns
  Note: A DVD set by the same name is also available. This Ken Burns production contains wonderful cinematography and really brings the Lewis and Clark expedition to life. Highly recommended if you have access to a copy and want to supplement the book.
- Book of Centuries (one for each student)

Note: We recommend that grades 10–12 students add an American Government course either during the Modern Times study next year or complete part of it this year and part of it next year.

Optional Resources
- Dover coloring books

Colonial and Early American Fashions
Early American Crafts and Occupations
Early American Trades
Everyday Dress of the American Colonial Period
Life in Colonial America
Heroes and Heroines of the American Revolution
Story of the American Revolution
- Various resources for optional hands-on projects

World History, Bible, Geography Resources

- *Stories of the Nations, Volume 1*, by Charles Morris, Lorene Lambert, and Sonya Shafer
  Though written for the younger grades, these gentle introductions to famous men of the time period will make a nice Family spine, contribute some additional biographies and information, and help tie together the different characters the older students will be reading about.
- *GOAL Bible Study Journal* by Sonya Shafer
- *Bible*
- *Jesus Is Better: Lessons from Hebrews* by Sonya Shafer
- *Sailing Alone Around the World* by Joshua Slocum
- *Uncle Josh's Outline Map book or CD* by George and Hannah Wiggers (or other outline maps of South America, Australia, and Central America)
- Labeled world map

Grades 1–3
- *Good Queen Bess* by Diane Stanley
- *Bard of Avon* by Diane Stanley
- *Starry Messenger* by Peter Sis OR *Galileo's Leaning Tower Experiment* by Wendy Macdonald
  While both can easily be read in one sitting, *Starry Messenger* is more of an overview of Galileo's life. Some of the illustrations may be a bit intense for sensitive children. *Galileo's Leaning Tower Experiment* focuses on one incident in Galileo's life.
- *A Lion to Guard Us* by Clyde Robert Bulla
  Short, easy to read chapters based on a true story. The Historical Note at the end reveals that Shakespeare wrote a play about this event.
- *Dangerous Journey* by Oliver Hunkin
  A shortened version of *Pilgrim's Progress*, using John Bunyan's original words. The illustrations are more on the cartoon side and a couple may be too intense for sensitive children, so use with discretion.
- *Peter the Great* by Diane Stanley
- *Can't You Make Them Behave, King George?* by Jean Fritz
  Gives the life of King George and how England felt about the American Revolution.
- *Out of Darkness: The Story of Louis Braille* by Russell Freedman
  An interesting biography of Louis Braille and his work in the early 1800s to help blind people read and write easily.

Grades 4–6
- *Good Queen Bess* by Diane Stanley
- *Bard of Avon* by Diane Stanley OR *Shakespeare and Macbeth: The Story Behind the Play* by Stewart Ross
  Both books give a great picture of what life was like in Shakespeare's time. *Shakespeare and Macbeth* spends several pages telling the story of the play Macbeth, which involves witches and murder. Use with discretion.
- *Along Came Galileo* by Jeanne Bendick
  Note: Be aware that Bendick states that Kepler believed in astrology (p. 41) and explains that a nova was light from a sun that had exploded "millions of years before" (p. 42). The rest of the book is well worth

reading, so just be prepared to discuss those two points with your child.

- *Strangers in the Land* by Louise A. Vernon

    One of Vernon's historical fiction works that bring church history to life. This one is about the Huguenots.
- *The Ocean of Truth: The Story of Sir Isaac Newton* by Joyce McPherson

    Joyce is a homeschooling mother and emphasizes the Christian beliefs of Newton.
- *The Story of Napoleon* by H. E. Marshall

Grades 7–9

- *Famous Men of the 16th and 17th Century* by Robert G. Shearer
- *Kidnapped* by Robert Louis Stevenson
- *The World of William Penn* by Genevieve Foster
- *Hearts and Hands: Chronicles of the Awakening Church* by Mindy and Brandon Withrow
- *The Year of the Horseless Carriage* by Genevieve Foster
- *The Story of Modern France* by H. A. Guerber

    Only chapters 1–23, covering the French Revolution, will be used from this resource, which is available free online.
- *Lafayette and the American Revolution* by Russell Freedman
- *Discovering Doctrine* by Sonya Shafer (one for each student)
- Book of Centuries (one for each student)

    Note: *As of the writing of this handbook,* Famous Men of the 18th Century *was not yet available. When it is released, you could add it to the schedule or substitute it for the two Genevieve Foster books.*

Grades 10–12

- *Famous Men of the 16th and 17th Century* by Robert G. Shearer
- *Waverley, Volume 1,* by Walter Scott
- *The World of William Penn* by Genevieve Foster
- *Hearts and Hands: Chronicles of the Awakening Church* by Mindy and Brandon Withrow
- "Sinners in the Hands of an Angry God" by Jonathan Edwards

    If you already have a copy of *American Voices*, you will find the sermon on pages 20–29, or you can easily find it online by doing an Internet search.
- *The Year of the Horseless Carriage* by Genevieve Foster
- *A Tale of Two Cities* by Charles Dickens
- *Lafayette and the American Revolution* by Russell Freedman
- *Discovering Doctrine* by Sonya Shafer (one for each student)
- Book of Centuries (one for each student)

    Note: *As of the writing of this handbook,* Famous Men of the 18th Century *was not yet available. When it is released, you could add it to the schedule or substitute it for the two Genevieve Foster books.*

Optional Resources

- *Master Skylark* by John Bennett

    A living picture of England during the days of Queen Elizabeth and Shakespeare, with appearances by both. Enough plot twists to keep the interest of the whole family, yet innocent enough for the young ones. Highly recommended as a Family read-aloud.
- Dover coloring books

    Tudor and Elizabethan Fashions

    French Baroque and Rococo Fashions

**Visit our CM Bookfinder at http://apps.simplycharlottemason.com/
for more information on each book, including where to find it.**

Term 1

(12 weeks; 5 lessons/week)

American History Resources

- *Stories of America, Volume 1*, by Charles Morris and Sonya Shafer

Grades 1–3

- *The Pilgrims of Plimoth* by Marcia Sewall
- *Samuel Eaton's Day: A Day in the Life of a Pilgrim Boy* by Kate Waters
- *Sarah Morton's Day: A Day in the Life of a Pilgrim Girl* by Kate Waters
- *Tapenum's Day: A Wampanoag Indian Boy in Pilgrim Times* by Kate Waters
- *The Courage of Sarah Noble* by Alice Dalgliesh

Grades 4–6

- *The Landing of the Pilgrims* by James Daugherty

Grades 7–9

- *Poor Richard* by James Daugherty
- Book of Centuries (one for each student)

Grades 10–12

- *The Autobiography of Benjamin Franklin* by Benjamin Franklin
- *American Voices* edited by Ray Notgrass
- Book of Centuries (one for each student)

Optional Resources

- Dover coloring books
  Colonial and Early American Fashions
  Early American Crafts and Occupations
  Early American Trades
  Everyday Dress of the American Colonial Period
  Life in Colonial America
- Various resources for optional hands-on projects

World History, Bible, Geography Resources

- *Stories of the Nations, Volume 1*, by Charles Morris, Lorene Lambert, and Sonya Shafer
- *GOAL Bible Study Journal* by Sonya Shafer
- Bible
- *Sailing Alone Around the World* by Joshua Slocum
- *Uncle Josh's Outline Map book or CD* by George and Hannah Wiggers (or other outline map of South America)
- Labeled world map

Grades 1–3

- *Good Queen Bess* by Diane Stanley
- *Bard of Avon* by Diane Stanley
- *Starry Messenger* by Peter Sis OR *Galileo's Leaning Tower Experiment* by Wendy Macdonald
- *A Lion to Guard Us* by Clyde Robert Bulla

Grades 4–6

- *Good Queen Bess* by Diane Stanley

- *Bard of Avon* by Diane Stanley OR *Shakespeare and Macbeth: The Story Behind the Play* by Stewart Ross
- *Along Came Galileo* by Jeanne Bendick

Grades 7–9
- *Famous Men of the 16th and 17th Century* by Robert G. Shearer
- *Discovering Doctrine* by Sonya Shafer (one for each student)
- Book of Centuries (one for each student)

Grades 10–12
- *Famous Men of the 16th and 17th Century* by Robert G. Shearer
- *Discovering Doctrine* by Sonya Shafer (one for each student)
- Book of Centuries (one for each student)

Optional Resources
- *Master Skylark*
- Dover coloring book
  Tudor and Elizabethan Fashions

	Family	Grades 1–3	Grades 4–6	Grades 7–9	Grades 10–12
Week 1					
Bible	Ephesians 1				
World History	Stories of the Nations, Vol. 1, ch. 1, 2; (opt.) Master Skylark, ch. 1, 2			Famous Men of the 16th and 17th Century, ch. 1, 2	Famous Men of the 16th and 17th Century, ch. 1, 2
Geography	Sailing Alone Around the World, ch. 1; Map Drill: South America				
American History	Stories of America, Vol. 1, ch. 1, 2		The Landing of the Pilgrims, pp. 1–9 ✓	Poor Richard, ch. 1	The Autobiography of Ben Franklin; American Voices, p. 1
Week 2					
Bible	Ephesians 2				
World History	Stories of the Nations, Vol. 1, ch. 3; (opt.) Master Skylark, ch. 3–5	Good Queen Bess ✓	Good Queen Bess ✓	Famous Men of the 16th and 17th Century, ch. 3, 4	Famous Men of the 16th and 17th Century, ch. 3, 4
Geography	Sailing Alone Around the World, ch. 2; Map Drill: South America				
American History	Stories of America, Vol. 1, ch. 3		The Landing of the Pilgrims, pp. 10–17	Poor Richard, ch. 2, 3	The Autobiography of Ben Franklin; American Voices, p. 2
Week 3					
Bible	Ephesians 3				
World History	(opt.) Master Skylark, ch. 6–9	Good Queen Bess ✓	Good Queen Bess ✓	Famous Men of the 16th and 17th Century, ch. 5, 6	Famous Men of the 16th and 17th Century, ch. 5, 6
Geography	Sailing Alone Around the World, ch. 3A; Map Drill: South America				
American History		The Pilgrims of Plimoth, sections 1, 2	The Landing of the Pilgrims, pp. 18–31	Poor Richard, ch. 4, 5	The Autobiography of Ben Franklin
Week 4					
Bible	Ephesians 4				
World History	Stories of the Nations, Vol. 1, ch. 4; (opt.) Master Skylark, ch. 10–12	Good Queen Bess; ✓ Bard of Avon ✓	Good Queen Bess; ✓ Bard of Avon OR Shakespeare and Macbeth, pp. 7–13	Famous Men of the 16th and 17th Century, ch. 7, 8	Famous Men of the 16th and 17th Century, ch. 7, 8
Geography	Sailing Alone Around the World, ch. 3B; Map Drill: South America				
American History		The Pilgrims of ✓ Plimoth, sections 3–5	The Landing of the Pilgrims, pp. 35–55	Poor Richard, ch. 6, 7	The Autobiography of Ben Franklin

	Family	Grades 1–3	Grades 4–6	Grades 7–9	Grades 10–12
Week 5					
Bible	Ephesians 5				
World History	(opt.) Master Skylark, ch. 13–16	Bard of Avon	Bard of Avon OR Shakespeare and Macbeth, pp. 14–31	Famous Men of the 16th and 17th Century, ch. 9, 10	Famous Men of the 16th and 17th Century, ch. 9, 10
Geography	Sailing Alone Around the World, ch. 4A; Map Drill: South America				
American History		Samuel Eaton's Day; Sarah Morton's Day	The Landing of the Pilgrims, pp. 56–73	Poor Richard, ch. 8, 9	The Autobiography of Ben Franklin
Week 6					
Bible	Ephesians 6				
World History	(opt.) Master Skylark, ch. 17–20	Bard of Avon, pp.	Bard of Avon, pp. OR Shakespeare and Macbeth, pp. 32–end	Famous Men of the 16th and 17th Century, ch. 11, 12	Famous Men of the 16th and 17th Century, ch. 11, 12
Geography	Sailing Alone Around the World, ch. 4B; Map Drill: South America				
American History	Stories of America, Vol. 1, ch. 4, 5		The Landing of the Pilgrims, pp. 74–81	Poor Richard, ch. 10, 11	The Autobiography of Ben Franklin; American Voices, pp. 6–9
Week 7					
Bible	Philippians 1, 2				
World History	Stories of the Nations, Vol. 1, ch. 5, 6; (opt.) Master Skylark, ch. 21–24	Starry Messenger OR Galileo's Leaning Tower Experiment	Along Came Galileo, ch. 1	Famous Men of the 16th and 17th Century, ch. 13	Famous Men of the 16th and 17th Century, ch. 13
Geography	Sailing Alone Around the World, ch. 5A; Map Drill: South America				
American History	Stories of America, Vol. 1, ch. 6, 7		The Landing of the Pilgrims, pp. 85–93	Poor Richard, ch. 12, 13	The Autobiography of Ben Franklin; American Voices, pp. 10–19
Week 8					
Bible	Philippians 3, 4				
World History	Stories of the Nations, Vol. 1, ch. 7; (opt.) Master Skylark, ch. 25–27	A Lion to Guard Us, ch. 1–6	Along Came Galileo, ch. 2, 3	Famous Men of the 16th and 17th Century, ch. 14, 15	Famous Men of the 16th and 17th Century, ch. 14, 15
Geography	Sailing Alone Around the World, ch. 5B; Map Drill: South America				
American History	Stories of America, Vol. 1, ch. 8, 9		The Landing of the Pilgrims, pp. 94–105	Poor Richard, ch. 14, 15	The Autobiography of Ben Franklin

	Family	Grades 1–3	Grades 4–6	Grades 7–9	Grades 10–12
Week 9					
Bible	Colossians 1, 2				
World History	(opt.) Master Skylark, ch. 28–31	A Lion to Guard Us, ch. 7–12 ✓	Along Came Galileo, ch. 4, 5	Famous Men of the 16th and 17th Century, ch. 16, 17	Famous Men of the 16th and 17th Century, ch. 16, 17
Geography	Sailing Alone Around the World, ch. 6A; Map Drill: South America				
American History	Stories of America, Vol. 1, ch. 10	Tapenum's Day; ✓ Courage of Sarah ✓ Noble, ch. 1	The Landing of the Pilgrims, pp. 106–117	Poor Richard, ch. 16, 17	The Autobiography of Ben Franklin; American Voices, pp. 30, 31
Week 10					
Bible	Colossians 3, 4				
World History	(opt.) Master Skylark, ch. 32–35	A Lion to Guard Us, ✓ ch. 13–18	Along Came Galileo, ch. 6, 7	Famous Men of the 16th and 17th Century, ch. 18, 19	Famous Men of the 16th and 17th Century, ch. 18, 19
Geography	Sailing Alone Around the World, ch. 6B; Map Drill: South America				
American History		Courage of Sarah ✓ Noble, ch. 2, 3	The Landing of the Pilgrims, pp. 118–138	Poor Richard, ch. 18, 19	The Autobiography of Ben Franklin
Week 11					
Bible	Philemon				
World History	(opt.) Master Skylark, ch. 36–39	A Lion to Guard Us, ✓ ch. 19–Historical Note	Along Came Galileo, ch. 8–11	Famous Men of the 16th and 17th Century, ch. 20, 21	Famous Men of the 16th and 17th Century, ch. 20, 21
Geography	Sailing Alone Around the World, ch. 7A; Map Drill: South America				
American History		Courage of Sarah ✓ Noble, ch. 4, 5	The Landing of the Pilgrims, pp. 139–149	Poor Richard, ch. 20 and Catch up	The Autobiography of Ben Franklin, finish
Week 12					
Bible	Exam				
World History	Exam			Famous Men of the 16th and 17th Century, ch. 22	Famous Men of the 16th and 17th Century, ch. 22
Geography	Sailing Alone Around the World, ch. 7B				
American History	Exam or Project		Catch up		Catch up

Lesson 1: Columbus, the Great Sailor

Materials Needed
- *Stories of America, Volume 1*
- *The Landing of the Pilgrims* (grades 4–6)
- *The Autobiography of Benjamin Franklin* (grades 10–12)

Family: Ask students what they recall about Christopher Columbus from previous studies. Explain that you will be starting a history of America and this history begins with Columbus. Write "Columbus" on a sheet of paper or small whiteboard so students can see how it is spelled. Read together *Stories of America, Volume 1*, chapter 1, "Columbus, the Great Sailor," and ask for an oral narration.

Columbus arrives in America (1492)

   Read together the poem "Columbus" from *Stories of America, Volume 1*, pages 15 and 16.

Grades 4–6: Read with your older children or assign as independent reading *The Landing of the Pilgrims*, pages 1–4. Ask for an oral or written narration.

Grades 10–12: Read with your older children or assign as independent reading about 7 pages of *The Autobiography of Benjamin Franklin*, from the salutation through the account of the stone wharf. Ask for an oral or written narration.

 ## Lesson 2: Captain John Smith and  Jamestown

Materials Needed
- *Stories of America, Volume 1*
- *The Landing of the Pilgrims* (grades 4–6)
- *Poor Richard* (grades 7–9)
- *The Autobiography of Benjamin Franklin* (grades 10–12)
- *American Voices* (grades 10–12)

John Smith, Pocahontas, and Jamestown (1607)

Family: Ask students what they recall from last time's reading about Christopher Columbus. Explain that while Spain and France were eager to send people to live in the New World that Columbus had discovered, England took its time. Write "John Smith," "Pocahontas," and "Jamestown" on a sheet of paper or small whiteboard. Read together *Stories of America, Volume 1*, chapter 2, "Captain John Smith and Jamestown," and ask for an oral narration.

   Locate Virginia on the map on page 181. Read together the poem "Pocahontas" on pages 23 and 24.

Grades 4–6: Read with your older children or assign as independent reading *The Landing of the Pilgrims,* pages 5–9. Ask for an oral or written narration.

Grades 7–9: Read with your older children or assign as independent reading *Poor Richard,* chapter 1. Ask for an oral or written narration.

Grades 10–12: Read with your older children or assign as independent reading about 7 pages of *The Autobiography of Benjamin Franklin,* from the description of his father through his critique of Pope's poetry. Ask for an oral or written narration.

Also read with your older children or assign as independent reading *American Voices,* page 1, "A Description of New England."

Reminder: Get the book The Pilgrims of Plimouth *for grades 1–3 for lesson 11.*

 ## Lesson 3: A Blue-Nose Ancestry & Ephesians 1

Materials Needed
- *Sailing Alone Around the World*
- Outline map of South America; labeled world map
- Bible
- *GOAL Bible Study Journal*
- *Discovering Doctrine* (grades 7–12)

Family Geography Book: Read together *Sailing Alone Around the World,* chapter 1, and ask for an oral narration.

Tip: If the sailing jargon gets to be too distracting from the story line, feel free to skip those details as you read aloud.

Family Map Drill: Give each student a copy of a blank outline map of South America. Encourage them to label all the countries that they know on the map. (Don't worry if they don't know any yet. They will soon.) Compare their labeled countries with a labeled world map and make any necessary corrections. Then have them label two or three more countries on their maps, copying the spelling and locations from the labeled world map.

Family Bible Study: Read together Ephesians 1, looking for any descriptions of promises, commands, sins, or principles, as explained in your *GOAL Bible Study Journal*:

Grasp this promise.
Obey this command.
Avoid this sin.
Live this principle.

Record your findings in your *GOAL Bible Study Journal*.

Tip: Older students should also be listening for doctrinal truths that they can add to their ongoing Discovering Doctrine books.

Tip: Be sure to review your GOAL findings each day of the week in order to help keep them in the forefront of everyone's minds. You won't see reminders in every lesson in this book, so set a time now that will work best for a quick read-through each day.

Tip: If you would like to download a free bookmark that will remind you of the GOAL items to look for in a passage, visit http:// simplycharlottemason.com/books/goal-bible-study-journal/links-tips/ You might want to print a bookmark for each child, so he can refer to it during your family Bible study times.

Lesson 4: A Bird's-Eye View

Materials Needed
- *Stories of the Nations, Volume 1*
- (optional) *Master Skylark*
- *Famous Men of the 16th and 17th Century* (grades 7–12)

Family: Explain that while you are studying the history of your country, you also want to study what was happening in the rest of the world. The other countries and people were not standing still doing nothing during those same years. Read together *Stories of the Nations, Volume 1*, chapter 1, "A Bird's-Eye View." You may want to refer to the map on page 165 if your child is not familiar with the continents and countries mentioned.

Tip: The maps in the back of Stories of the Nations *will prove helpful as you read the book. The chapters mention more than 100 geographical locations as part of the stories, and your child will learn much about geography by simply finding those places as you read about what happened there.*

Optional Family Read-Aloud: Read together *Master Skylark*, chapter 1, "The Lord Admiral's Players."

Grades 7–12: Read with your older children or assign as independent reading *Famous Men of the 16th and 17th Century,* chapter 1, "Catherine de' Medici." Ask for an oral or written narration.

Reminder: Get the book Good Queen Bess *for grades 1–6 for lesson 9.*

Lesson 5: How the Ottomans Disappeared

Materials Needed
- *Stories of the Nations, Volume 1*
- (optional) *Master Skylark*
- *Famous Men of the 16th and 17th Century* (grades 7–12)

Family: Write "Ottomans" on a small white board or sheet of paper. Read together *Stories of the Nations, Volume 1*, chapter 2, "How the Ottomans Disappeared." Use the map on page 165, or another world map, to find Turkey as described in the chapter. Ask for an oral narration.

Optional Family Read-Aloud: Read together *Master Skylark*, chapter 2, "Nicholas Attwood's Home."

Grades 7–12: Read with your older children or assign as independent reading *Famous Men of the 16th and 17th Century*, chapter 2, "Henry of Navarre." Ask for an oral or written narration.

Tip: Make sure older children are up to date with their Book of Centuries entries.

Lesson 6: Captain Miles Standish and the Pilgrims

Materials Needed
- *Stories of America, Volume 1*
- *The Landing of the Pilgrims* (grades 4–6)
- *Poor Richard* (grades 7–9)
- *The Autobiography of Benjamin Franklin* (grades 10–12)
- *American Voices* (grades 10–12)

Miles Standish and the Pilgrims (1620)

Family: Ask students what they recall from last time's reading about Captain John Smith, Pocahontas, and Jamestown. Explain that people decided to leave England and make the trip to live in the New World for many different reasons. Write "Pilgrims" and "Miles Standish" on a sheet of paper or small whiteboard. Read together *Stories of America, Volume 1*, chapter 3, "Captain Miles Standish and the Pilgrims," and ask for an oral narration.

Locate Massachusetts on the map on page 181 and explain that Plymouth was in that area.

Grades 4–6: Read with your older children or assign as independent reading *The Landing of the Pilgrims*, pages 10–14. Ask for an oral or written narration.

Grades 7–9: Read with your older children or assign as independent reading *Poor Richard,* chapter 2. Ask for an oral or written narration.

Grades 10–12: Read with your older children or assign as independent reading about 7 pages of *The Autobiography of Benjamin Franklin,* from his working for his brother's newspaper through his landing at Market Street wharf near Philadelphia. Ask for an oral or written narration.

Also read with your older children or assign as independent reading *American Voices,* page 2, "Mayflower Compact." Ask for a narration, summarizing the purpose and contents of that written contract.

 # Lesson 7: The Landing of the Pilgrim Fathers

Materials Needed
- *Stories of America, Volume 1*
- *The Landing of the Pilgrims* (grades 4–6)
- *Poor Richard* (grades 7–9)
- *The Autobiography of Benjamin Franklin* (grades 10–12)

Family: Ask students what they recall from last time's reading about Captain Miles Standish and the Pilgrims. Explain that today's poem summarizes, in picturesque language, why the Pilgrims came to America. Read together the poem "The Landing of the Pilgrim Fathers" from *Stories of America, Volume 1,* pages 29 and 30.

Grades 4–6: Read with your older children or assign as independent reading *The Landing of the Pilgrims,* pages 15–17. Ask for an oral or written narration.

Grades 7–9: Read with your older children or assign as independent reading *Poor Richard,* chapter 3. Ask for an oral or written narration.

Grades 10–12: Read with your older children or assign as independent reading about 7 pages of *The Autobiography of Benjamin Franklin,* from his first entry into Philadelphia through his father's counsel and advice to return to Philadelphia. Ask for an oral or written narration.

 # Lesson 8: Failure as a Fisherman & Ephesians 2

Materials Needed
- *Sailing Alone Around the World*
- Outline map of South America; labeled world map
- Bible

• *GOAL Bible Study Journal*
• *Discovering Doctrine* (grades 7–12)

Family Geography Book: Ask students what they recall about Joshua Slocum and *The Spray*. Read together *Sailing Alone Around the World*, chapter 2, and ask for an oral narration.

Tip: Use a labeled world map to trace Slocum's voyage as you read.

Family Map Drill: Give each student a copy of an outline map of South America. Encourage them to label all the countries that they know on the map. Compare their labeled countries with a labeled world map and make any necessary corrections. Then have them label two or three more countries on their maps, copying the spelling and locations from the labeled world map.

Tip: Allow students to also label bodies of water, rivers, and mountains if they want to.

Family Bible Study: Review your findings from last time and note how many of those items family members were able to put into practice during the week. Thank God for bringing His Word to your minds and giving you the strength to be doers, not just a hearers. Read together Ephesians 2, looking for any descriptions of promises, commands, sins, or principles, as explained in your *GOAL Bible Study Journal*:

Grasp this promise.
Obey this command.
Avoid this sin.
Live this principle.

Record your findings in your *GOAL Bible Study Journal*. Older students should also be listening for doctrinal truths that they can add to their ongoing *Discovering Doctrine* books.

Lesson 9: Queen Elizabeth and the Little Ships

Materials Needed
• *Stories of the Nations, Volume 1*
• (optional) *Master Skylark*
• *Good Queen Bess* (grades 1–6)
• *Famous Men of the 16th and 17th Century* (grades 7–12)

Queen Elizabeth rules England (1558–1603)

Family: Ask students what they recall from last time's reading about the Ottomans. Explain that while the Ottomans were ruling in Turkey, other events were happening in England. Read together *Stories of the Nations, Volume 1*, chapter 3, "Queen Elizabeth and the Little Ships." Use the map on page 155 to locate England and Spain and see what Europe looked like during Queen Elizabeth's reign. (Note: No narration will be required here because all the students will begin to read and narrate about Queen Elizabeth more in-depth in their additional reading today.)

Optional Family Read-Aloud: Read together *Master Skylark*, chapter 3, "The Last Straw."

Grades 1–6: Read together *Good Queen Bess*, to the bottom of the sixth page that ends with the "Elizabeth learned very early to choose her friends carefully" sentence. Ask for an oral narration.

Grades 7–12: Read with your older children or assign as independent reading *Famous Men of the 16th and 17th Century*, chapter 3, "Elizabeth I." Ask for an oral or written narration.

Lesson 10: Elizabethan Era, part 1

Materials Needed
- (optional) *Master Skylark*
- *Good Queen Bess* (grades 1–6)
- *Famous Men of the 16th and 17th Century* (grades 7–12)

Optional Family Read-Aloud: Read together *Master Skylark*, chapters 4 and 5, "Off for Coventry" and "In the Warwick Road."

Grades 1–6: Ask students what they recall from last time's reading about Elizabeth's father, King Henry VIII. Read together *Good Queen Bess*, from "Edward—the son Henry had risked so much to have" to the bottom of six more pages, ending with the "Still, Leicester was her lifelong good friend" sentence. Ask for an oral narration.

Grades 7–12: Read with your older children or assign as independent reading *Famous Men of the 16th and 17th Century*, chapter 4, "Sir Francis Drake." Ask for an oral or written narration.

Reminder: Get the book Bard of Avon *for grades 1–3 for lesson 20. You may use* Bard of Avon *for grades 4–6 also or get* Shakespeare and Macbeth. *See page 16 for details that might help you decide which to use.*

Tip: Make sure older children are up to date with their Book of Centuries entries.

Lesson 11: Colonial Times, part 1

Materials Needed
- *The Pilgrims of Plimoth* (grades 1–3)
- *The Landing of the Pilgrims* (grades 4–6)
- *Poor Richard* (grades 7–9)
- *The Autobiography of Benjamin Franklin* (grades 10–12)

Grades 1–3: Read together *The Pilgrims of Plimoth*, section 1, "The Pilgrims." Ask for an oral narration if desired.

Grades 4–6: Read with your older children or assign as independent reading *The Landing of the Pilgrims,* pages 18–23. Ask for an oral or written narration.

Grades 7–9: Read with your older children or assign as independent reading *Poor Richard,* chapter 4. Ask for an oral or written narration.

Grades 10–12: Read with your older children or assign as independent reading about 7 pages of *The Autobiography of Benjamin Franklin,* from his visit to his brother John through the trick they played on Ralph. Ask for an oral or written narration.

Reminder: Get the books Samuel Eaton's Day *and* Sarah Morton's Day *for grades 1–3 for lessons 21 and 22.*

Lesson 12: Colonial Times, part 2

Materials Needed
- *The Pilgrims of Plimoth* (grades 1–3)
- *The Landing of the Pilgrims* (grades 4–6)
- *Poor Richard* (grades 7–9)
- *The Autobiography of Benjamin Franklin* (grades 10–12)

Grades 1–3: Read together *The Pilgrims of Plimoth*, section 2, "Menfolk." Ask for an oral narration if desired.

Grades 4–6: Read with your older children or assign as independent reading *The Landing of the Pilgrims,* pages 24–31. Ask for an oral or written narration.

Grades 7–9: Read with your older children or assign as independent reading *Poor Richard,* chapter 5. Ask for an oral or written narration.

Grades 10–12: Read with your older children or assign as independent reading about 7 pages of *The Autobiography of Benjamin Franklin,* from his frequent visits to the governor's house through his getting on fair footing with the pressmen at Watt's. Ask for an oral or written narration.

Lesson 13: Good-by to the American Coast & Ephesians 3

Materials Needed
- *Sailing Alone Around the World*
- Outline map of South America; labeled world map
- Bible
- *GOAL Bible Study Journal*
- *Discovering Doctrine* (grades 7–12)

Family Geography Book: See if students can trace on the labeled world map from Boston to Gloucester to Nova Scotia. Ask students what they recall about Joshua Slocum's trip so far. Read together *Sailing Alone Around the World*, the first half of chapter 3, and ask for an oral narration.

Tip: Be sure to follow Joshua Slocum's voyage on a world map.

Family Map Drill: Give each student a copy of an outline map of South America. Encourage them to label all the countries that they know on the map. Compare their labeled countries with a labeled world map and make any necessary corrections. Then have them label two or three more countries on their maps, copying the spelling and locations from the labeled world map.

Family Bible Study: Review your findings from last time and note how many of those items family members were able to put into practice during the week. Thank God for bringing His Word to your minds and giving you the strength to be doers, not just a hearers. Read together Ephesians 3, looking for any descriptions of promises, commands, sins, or principles. Record your findings in your *GOAL Bible Study Journal*. Older students should also be listening for doctrinal truths that they can add to their ongoing *Discovering Doctrine* books.

Lesson 14: Elizabethan Era, part 2

Materials Needed
- (optional) *Master Skylark*
- *Good Queen Bess* (grades 1–6)
- *Famous Men of the 16th and 17th Century* (grades 7–12)

Optional Family Read-Aloud: Read together *Master Skylark*, chapters 6 and 7, "The Master-Player" and "Well Sung, Master Skylark!"

Grades 1–6: Ask students what they recall from last time's reading about how Elizabeth became queen and how she dealt with people and countries. Read together *Good Queen Bess*, from "When Elizabeth was twenty-nine" to the bottom of six more pages, ending with the "Mary would spend the rest of her life being shuttled" sentence. Ask for an oral narration.

Grades 7–12: Read with your older children or assign as independent reading *Famous Men of the 16th and 17th Century,* chapter 5, "Sir Walter Raleigh." Ask for an oral or written narration.

 Lesson 15: Elizabethan Era, part 3

Materials Needed
- (optional) *Master Skylark*
- *Good Queen Bess* (grades 1–6)
- *Famous Men of the 16th and 17th Century* (grades 7–12)

Optional Family Read-Aloud: Read together *Master Skylark,* chapters 8 and 9, "The Admiral's Company" and "The May-Day Play."

Grades 1–6: Ask students what they recall from last time's reading about Elizabeth's tours and her cousin Mary. Read together *Good Queen Bess,* from "Mary had not been imprisoned long" to the bottom of six more pages, ending with the "She wrote dangerous answers" sentence. Ask for an oral narration.

Grades 7–12: Read with your older children or assign as independent reading *Famous Men of the 16th and 17th Century,* chapter 6, "James I." Ask for an oral or written narration.

Tip: Make sure older children are up to date with their Book of Centuries entries.

 Lesson 16: Colonial Times, part 3

Materials Needed
- *The Pilgrims of Plimoth* (grades 1–3)
- *The Landing of the Pilgrims* (grades 4–6)
- *Poor Richard* (grades 7–9)
- *The Autobiography of Benjamin Franklin* (grades 10–12)

Grades 1–3: Read together *The Pilgrims of Plimoth,* section 3, "Womenfolk." Ask for an oral narration if desired.

Grades 4–6: Read with your older children or assign as independent reading *The Landing of the Pilgrims,* pages 35–45. Ask for an oral or written narration.

Grades 7–9: Read with your older children or assign as independent reading *Poor Richard,* chapter 6. Ask for an oral or written narration.

Grades 10–12: Read with your older children or assign as independent reading about 7 pages of *The Autobiography of Benjamin Franklin,* from his moving to Dukestreet through his being uneasy about his debt to Vernon. Ask for an oral or written narration.

Lesson 17: Colonial Times, part 4

Materials Needed
- *The Pilgrims of Plimoth* (grades 1–3)
- *The Landing of the Pilgrims* (grades 4–6)
- *Poor Richard* (grades 7–9)
- *The Autobiography of Benjamin Franklin* (grades 10–12)

Grades 1–3: Read together *The Pilgrims of Plimoth*, sections 4 and 5, "Children and Youngfolk" and "The Plantation." Ask for an oral narration if desired.

Grades 4–6: Read with your older children or assign as independent reading *The Landing of the Pilgrims,* pages 46–55. Ask for an oral or written narration.

Grades 7–9: Read with your older children or assign as independent reading *Poor Richard,* chapter 7. Ask for an oral or written narration.

Grades 10–12: Read with your older children or assign as independent reading about 7 pages of *The Autobiography of Benjamin Franklin,* from his contriving a mould for types through the introduction of the members of the JUNTO club. Ask for an oral or written narration.

Lesson 18: Arrival at the Azores & Ephesians 4

Materials Needed
- *Sailing Alone Around the World*
- Outline map of South America; labeled world map
- Bible
- *GOAL Bible Study Journal*
- *Discovering Doctrine* (grades 7–12)

Family Geography Book: Ask students what they recall about Joshua Slocum's first few days in the Atlantic. Read together *Sailing Alone Around the World*, the last half of chapter 3, and ask for an oral narration. See if students can trace on the world map from Boston to Nova Scotia to the Azores.

Family Map Drill: Give each student a copy of an outline map of South America. Encourage them to label all the countries that they know on the map. Compare their labeled countries with a labeled world map and make any necessary corrections. Then have them label two or three more countries on their maps, copying the spelling and locations from the labeled world map.

Family Bible Study: Review your findings from last time then read together Ephesians 4, looking for any descriptions of promises, commands, sins, or principles. Record your findings in your *GOAL Bible Study Journal*. Older students should also be listening for doctrinal truths that they can add to their ongoing *Discovering Doctrine* books.

Lesson 19: Elizabethan Era, part 4

Materials Needed
- (optional) *Master Skylark*
- *Good Queen Bess* (grades 1–6)
- *Famous Men of the 16th and 17th Century* (grades 7–12)

Optional Family Read-Aloud: Read together *Master Skylark*, chapters 10 and 11, "After the Play" and "Disowned."

Grades 1–6: Ask students what they recall from last time's reading about Elizabeth and her cousin Mary. Read together *Good Queen Bess*, from "Walsingham's net caught many fish" to the end of the book. Ask for an oral narration.

Grades 7–12: Read with your older children or assign as independent reading *Famous Men of the 16th and 17th Century,* chapter 7, "Matteo Ricci." Ask for an oral or written narration.

Lesson 20: William Shakespeare and His Words

Materials Needed
- *Stories of the Nations, Volume 1*
- (optional) *Master Skylark*
- *Bard of Avon* (grades 1–3)
- *Bard of Avon* OR *Shakespeare and Macbeth* (grades 4–6)
- *Famous Men of the 16th and 17th Century* (grades 7–12)

William Shakespeare, English playwright (1564–1616)

Family: Write "Shakespeare" on a small white board or sheet of paper. If students have read any of Shakespeare's plays, discuss what they thought of those plays and which ones were their favorites. Read together *Stories of the Nations, Volume 1*, chapter 4, "William Shakespeare and His Words." (Note: No narration will be required from this book because all the students will begin to read and narrate about Shakespeare more in-depth in their additional reading today.)

Optional Family Read-Aloud: Read together *Master Skylark*, chapter 12, "A Strange Ride."

Grades 1–3: Read together *Bard of Avon*, from the beginning through four pages of text ("In the year 1569" through "It does not appear that they had a very happy marriage"). Ask for an oral narration.

Grades 4–6: Read together *Bard of Avon*, as described for grades 1–3, OR *Shakespeare and Macbeth*, pages 7–13. Ask for an oral narration.

Grades 7–12: Read with your older children or assign as independent reading *Famous Men of the 16th and 17th Century*, chapter 8, "William Shakespeare." Ask for an oral or written narration.

Tip: Make sure older children are up to date with their Book of Centuries entries.

 Lesson 21: Colonial Times, part 5

Materials Needed
- *Samuel Eaton's Day* (grades 1–3)
- *The Landing of the Pilgrims* (grades 4–6)
- *Poor Richard* (grades 7–9)
- *The Autobiography of Benjamin Franklin* (grades 10–12)

Grades 1–3: Read together *Samuel Eaton's Day*.

Grades 4–6: Read with your older children or assign as independent reading *The Landing of the Pilgrims*, pages 56–64. Ask for an oral or written narration.

Grades 7–9: Read with your older children or assign as independent reading *Poor Richard*, chapter 8. Ask for an oral or written narration.

Grades 10–12: Read with your older children or assign as independent reading about 7 pages of *The Autobiography of Benjamin Franklin*, from the business those club members sent his way through the end of Part One. Ask for an oral or written narration.

Lesson 22: Colonial Times, part 6

Materials Needed
- *Sarah Morton's Day* (grades 1–3)
- *The Landing of the Pilgrims* (grades 4–6)
- *Poor Richard* (grades 7–9)
- *The Autobiography of Benjamin Franklin* (grades 10–12)

Grades 1–3: Read together *Sarah Morton's Day.*

Grades 4–6: Read with your older children or assign as independent reading *The Landing of the Pilgrims,* pages 65–73. Ask for an oral or written narration.

Grades 7–9: Read with your older children or assign as independent reading *Poor Richard,* chapter 9. Ask for an oral or written narration.

Grades 10–12: Read with your older children or assign as independent reading about 7 pages of *The Autobiography of Benjamin Franklin,* from the continuation of his life, written in 1784, through his decision not to attend church anymore. Ask for an oral or written narration.

 # Lesson 23: Squally weather in the Azores & Ephesians 5

Materials Needed
- *Sailing Alone Around the World*
- Outline map of South America; labeled world map
- Bible
- *GOAL Bible Study Journal*
- *Discovering Doctrine* (grades 7–12)

Family Geography Book: See if students can trace on the world map from Boston to Nova Scotia to the Azores. Ask students what they recall about Joshua Slocum's trip so far. Read together *Sailing Alone Around the World,* the first half of chapter 4, and ask for an oral narration.

Family Map Drill: Give each student a copy of an outline map of South America. Encourage them to label all the countries that they know on the map. Compare their labeled countries with a labeled world map and make any necessary corrections. Then have them label two or three more countries on their maps, copying the spelling and locations from the labeled world map.

Family Bible Study: Review your findings from last time then read together Ephesians 5, looking for any descriptions of promises, commands, sins, or principles. Record your findings in your *GOAL Bible Study Journal.* Older students should also be listening for doctrinal truths that they can add to their ongoing *Discovering Doctrine* books.

Lesson 24: Shakespeare and Beyond, part 1

Materials Needed
- (optional) *Master Skylark*
- *Bard of Avon* (grades 1–3)
- *Bard of Avon* OR *Shakespeare and Macbeth* (grades 4–6)
- *Famous Men of the 16th and 17th Century* (grades 7–12)

Optional Family Read-Aloud: Read together *Master Skylark*, chapters 13 and 14, "A Dash for Freedom" and "At Bay."

Grades 1–3: Ask students what they recall from last time's reading about Shakespeare. Read together four more pages of text from *Bard of Avon* ("William Shakespeare went to London" through "where all the famous Elizabethan theaters were built"). Ask for an oral narration.

Grades 4–6: Ask students what they recall from last time's reading about Shakespeare. Read together *Bard of Avon*, as described for grades 1–3, OR *Shakespeare and Macbeth*, pages 14–21. Ask for an oral narration.

Grades 7–12: Read with your older children or assign as independent reading *Famous Men of the 16th and 17th Century,* chapter 9, "John Smith." Ask for an oral or written narration.

 # Lesson 25: Shakespeare and Beyond, part 2

Materials Needed
- (optional) *Master Skylark*
- *Bard of Avon* (grades 1–3)
- *Bard of Avon* OR *Shakespeare and Macbeth* (grades 4–6)
- *Famous Men of the 16th and 17th Century* (grades 7–12)

Optional Family Read-Aloud: Read together *Master Skylark*, chapters 15 and 16, "London Town" and "Ma'm'selle Cicely Carew."

Grades 1–3: Ask students what they recall from last time's reading about Shakespeare. Read together four more pages of text from *Bard of Avon* ("Each acting company had about twelve men" through "such a series of great parts to play!"). Ask for an oral narration.

Grades 4–6: Ask students what they recall from last time's reading about Shakespeare. Read together *Bard of Avon*, as described for grades 1–3, OR *Shakespeare and Macbeth*, pages 22–31. Ask for an oral narration.

Grades 7–12: Read with your older children or assign as independent

Book of Centuries Timeline

reading *Famous Men of the 16th and 17th Century*, chapter 10, "Albrecht von Wallenstein." Ask for an oral or written narration.

Reminder: Get the book Starry Messenger *OR* Galileo's Leaning Tower Experiment *for grades 1–3 and* Along Came Galileo *for grades 4–6 for lesson 35.*

Tip: Make sure older children are up to date with their Book of Centuries entries.

Lesson 26: Roger Williams and the Puritans

Materials Needed
- *Stories of America, Volume 1*
- *The Landing of the Pilgrims* (grades 4–6)
- *Poor Richard* (grades 7–9)
- *The Autobiography of Benjamin Franklin* (grades 10–12)
- *American Voices* (grades 10–12)

Roger Williams and the Puritans (1636)

Family: Ask students what they recall about the Pilgrims and their reasons for coming to America. Explain that today's reading will tell about another group of people who came. Write "Puritans" and "Roger Williams" on a sheet of paper or small whiteboard. Read together *Stories of America, Volume 1*, chapter 4, "Roger Williams and the Puritans," and ask for an oral narration.

Locate Rhode Island on the map on page 181. Explain that the Puritans used little rhymes to help teach their children how to read. Read together the "New England Primer Alphabet" from *Stories of America, Vol. 1*, pages 33–35.

Grades 4–6: Read with your older children or assign as independent reading *The Landing of the Pilgrims*, pages 74–76. Ask for an oral or written narration.

Grades 7–9: Read with your older children or assign as independent reading *Poor Richard*, chapter 10. Ask for an oral or written narration.

Grades 10–12: Read with your older children or assign as independent reading about 7 pages of *The Autobiography of Benjamin Franklin*, from his bold and arduous project toward moral perfection through his always carrying his little book with him. Ask for an oral or written narration.

Also read with your older children or assign as independent reading *American Voices*, pages 6–9, "Bay Psalm Book (excerpts)," "Poems by Anne Bradstreet," and "New England Primer (excerpts)."

Lesson 27: How the Dutch Came to America

Materials Needed
- *Stories of America, Volume 1*
- *The Landing of the Pilgrims* (grades 4–6)
- *Poor Richard* (grades 7–9)
- *The Autobiography of Benjamin Franklin* (grades 10–12)

Family: Ask students what they recall from last time's reading about Roger Williams and the Puritans. Explain that people from many countries came to America. Today's reading will be about a group from Holland. Find Holland on a world map and look at its distance from New York. Read together *Stories of America, Volume 1*, chapter 5, "How the Dutch Came to America," and ask for an oral narration.

Grades 4–6: Read with your older children or assign as independent reading *The Landing of the Pilgrims*, pages 77–81. Ask for an oral or written narration.

Grades 7–9: Read with your older children or assign as independent reading *Poor Richard*, chapter 11. Ask for an oral or written narration.

Grades 10–12: Read with your older children or assign as independent reading about 7 pages of *The Autobiography of Benjamin Franklin*, from his scheme of Order giving him the most trouble through The Society of the Free and Easy. Ask for an oral or written narration.

 ## Lesson 28: A picnic on the Morocco shore & Ephesians 6

Materials Needed
- *Sailing Alone Around the World*
- Outline map of South America; labeled world map
- Bible
- *GOAL Bible Study Journal*
- *Discovering Doctrine* (grades 7–12)

Family Geography Book: Ask students what they recall about Joshua Slocum's trip sailing from the Azores. Read together *Sailing Alone Around the World*, the last half of chapter 4, and ask for an oral narration. See if students can trace on the world map from Boston to Nova Scotia to the Azores to Gibraltar and Morocco.

Family Map Drill: Give each student a copy of an outline map of South America. Encourage them to label all the countries that they know on the map. Compare their labeled countries with a labeled world map and

Book of Centuries Timeline

The Dutch settle in New York (1609)

make any necessary corrections. Then have them label two or three more countries on their maps, copying the spelling and locations from the labeled world map.

Family Bible Study: Review your findings from last time then read together Ephesians 6, looking for any descriptions of promises, commands, sins, or principles. Record your findings in your *GOAL Bible Study Journal.* Older students should also be listening for doctrinal truths that they can add to their ongoing *Discovering Doctrine* books.

 # Lesson 29: Shakespeare and Beyond, part 3

Materials Needed
- (optional) *Master Skylark*
- *Bard of Avon* (grades 1–3)
- *Bard of Avon* OR *Shakespeare and Macbeth* (grades 4–6)
- *Famous Men of the 16th and 17th Century* (grades 7–12)

Optional Family Read-Aloud: Read together *Master Skylark*, chapters 17 and 18, "Carew's Offer" and "Master Heywood Protests."

Grades 1–3: Ask students what they recall from last time's reading about Shakespeare. Read together four more pages of text from *Bard of Avon* ("Shakespeare's histories were very popular" through "The queen was willing to believe that they hadn't done it for political reasons"). Ask for an oral narration.

Grades 4–6: Ask students what they recall from last time's reading about Shakespeare. Read together *Bard of Avon*, as described for grades 1–3, OR *Shakespeare and Macbeth*, pages 32 through the end. Ask for an oral narration.

Grades 7–12: Read with your older children or assign as independent reading *Famous Men of the 16th and 17th Century,* chapter 11, "Gustavus Adolphus." Ask for an oral or written narration.

Reminder: Get the book A Lion to Guard Us *for grades 1–3 for lesson 39.*

 # Lesson 30: Shakespeare and Beyond, part 4

Materials Needed
- (optional) *Master Skylark*

- *Bard of Avon* (grades 1–3)
- *Bard of Avon,* if using this book (grades 4–6)
- *Famous Men of the 16th and 17th Century* (grades 7–12)

Optional Family Read-Aloud: Read together *Master Skylark,* chapters 19 and 20, "The Rose Play-house" and "Disappointment."

Grades 1–3: Ask students what they recall from last time's reading about Shakespeare. Finish reading *Bard of Avon.* Ask for an oral narration.

Grades 4–6: Ask students what they recall from last time's reading about Shakespeare. Finish reading *Bard of Avon,* if you have been using this book. Ask for an oral narration.

Grades 7–12: Read with your older children or assign as independent reading *Famous Men of the 16th and 17th Century,* chapter 12, "Samuel de Champlain." Ask for an oral or written narration.

Tip: Make sure older children are up to date with their Book of Centuries entries.

Lesson 31: How the Quakers Came to America

Materials Needed
- *Stories of America, Volume 1*
- *The Landing of the Pilgrims* (grades 4–6)
- *Poor Richard* (grades 7–9)
- *The Autobiography of Benjamin Franklin* (grades 10–12)
- *American Voices* (grades 10–12)

Family: Ask students what they recall from last time's reading about how the Dutch came to America. Explain that yet another group came to escape religious persecution: the Quakers. Write "Pilgrims," "Puritans," "Quakers," and "William Penn" on a sheet of paper or small whiteboard. Read together *Stories of America, Volume 1,* chapter 6, "How the Quakers Came to America," and ask for an oral narration. Locate Philadelphia on the map on page 181.

Grades 4–6: Read with your older children or assign as independent reading *The Landing of the Pilgrims,* pages 85–87. Ask for an oral or written narration.

Grades 7–9: Read with your older children or assign as independent reading *Poor Richard,* chapter 12. Ask for an oral or written narration.

Grades 10–12: Read with your older children or assign as independent reading about 7 pages of *The Autobiography of Benjamin Franklin,* from his first publishing his Almanac through his accepting the position of

Quaker William Penn founds Pennsylvania (1682)

postmaster-general. Ask for an oral or written narration.

Also read with your older children or assign as independent reading *American Voices*, pages 10–19, "Sayings from Poor Richard's Almanack."

Reminder: Get Tapenum's Day *and* The Courage of Sarah Noble *for grades 1–3 for lessons 41 and 42.*

 # Lesson 32: Maryland

Materials Needed
- *Stories of America, Volume 1*
- *The Landing of the Pilgrims* (grades 4–6)
- *Poor Richard* (grades 7–9)
- *The Autobiography of Benjamin Franklin* (grades 10–12)

Family: Ask students what they recall from last time's reading about the Quakers and how they came to America. Explain that Catholics and Protestants in Europe were also being persecuted for their beliefs, each in turn, depending on who was ruling their country at the time. So many of them traveled to the New World, as well. Write "Cavalier" and "Maryland" on a sheet of paper or small whiteboard. Read together *Stories of America, Volume 1*, chapter 7, "Maryland," and ask for an oral narration. Locate Maryland on the map on page 181. (You will have to look closely, for its name is curved, with the *M* right above the last letter in *Virginia*.)

Lord Baltimore settles Maryland (1634)

Grades 4–6: Read with your older children or assign as independent reading *The Landing of the Pilgrims*, pages 88–93. Ask for an oral or written narration.

Grades 7–9: Read with your older children or assign as independent reading *Poor Richard*, chapter 13. Ask for an oral or written narration.

Grades 10–12: Read with your older children or assign as independent reading about 7 pages of *The Autobiography of Benjamin Franklin*, from his turning his thoughts to public affairs through his establishing several of his workmen with printing-house partnerships. Ask for an oral or written narration.

Lesson 33: Sailing from Gibraltar & Philippians 1 and 2

Materials Needed
- *Sailing Alone Around the World*
- Outline map of South America; labeled world map
- Bible

- *GOAL Bible Study Journal*
- *Discovering Doctrine* (grades 7–12)

Family Geography Book: See if students can trace on the world map from Boston to Nova Scotia to the Azores to Gibraltar and Morocco. Ask students what they recall about Joshua Slocum's trip to Gibraltar. Read together *Sailing Alone Around the World*, the first half of chapter 5, and ask for an oral narration.

Family Map Drill: Give each student a copy of an outline map of South America. Encourage them to label all the countries that they know on the map. Compare their labeled countries with a labeled world map and make any necessary corrections. Then have them label two or three more countries on their maps, copying the spelling and locations from the labeled world map.

Family Bible Study: Review your findings from last time then read together Philippians 1 and 2, looking for any descriptions of promises, commands, sins, or principles. Record your findings in your *GOAL Bible Study Journal*. Older students should also be listening for doctrinal truths that they can add to their ongoing *Discovering Doctrine* books.

Lesson 34: Johannes Kepler Explores the Heavens

Materials Needed
- *Stories of the Nations, Volume 1*
- (optional) *Master Skylark*
- *Famous Men of the 16th and 17th Century*, if needed to catch up (grades 7–12)

Family: Write "Kepler" on a small white board or sheet of paper. Read together *Stories of the Nations, Volume 1*, chapter 5, "Johannes Kepler Explores the Heavens." Use the map on page 155 to find the locations as they are mentioned. Ask for an oral narration.

Johannes Kepler calculates the planets' orbits (1571–1630)

Optional Family Read-Aloud: Read together *Master Skylark*, chapters 21 and 22, "The Children of Paul's" and "The Skylark's Song."

Grades 7–12: Use today to catch up on any assigned readings or narrations from *Famous Men of the 16th and 17th Century*.

Lesson 35: Galileo Continues the Work

Materials Needed
- *Stories of the Nations, Volume 1*

Galileo uses a telescope to learn
about the heavens (1564–1642)

• (optional) *Master Skylark*
• *Starry Messenger* OR *Galileo's Leaning Tower Experiment* (grades 1–3)
• *Along Came Galileo* (grades 4–6)
• *Famous Men of the 16th and 17th Century* (grades 7–12)

Family: Ask students what they recall from last time's reading about Johannes Kepler. Read together *Stories of the Nations, Volume 1,* chapter 6, "Galileo Continues the Work." Ask for an oral narration.

Optional Family Read-Aloud: Read together *Master Skylark*, chapters 23 and 24, "A New Life" and "The Making of a Player."

Grades 1–3: Read together *Starry Messenger* OR *Galileo's Leaning Tower Experiment.*

Grades 4–6: Read with your older children or assign as independent reading *Along Came Galileo*, chapter 1, "Along Came Galileo." Ask for an oral or written narration.

Grades 7–12: Read with your older children or assign as independent reading *Famous Men of the 16th and 17th Century,* chapter 13, "Galileo Galilei." Ask for an oral or written narration.

Tip: Make sure older children are up to date with their Book of Centuries entries.

 Lesson 36: The Carolinas

Materials Needed
• *Stories of America, Volume 1*
• *The Landing of the Pilgrims* (grades 4–6)
• *Poor Richard* (grades 7–9)
• *The Autobiography of Benjamin Franklin* (grades 10–12)

Settlers in the Carolinas (1660)

Family: Ask students what they recall from last time's reading about Maryland. Explain that there was more land yet to the south where no Europeans had settled. Look at the map on page 181 in *Stories of America, Volume 1,* and locate that land area. Read together chapter 8, "The Carolinas," and ask for an oral narration.

Grades 4–6: Read with your older children or assign as independent reading *The Landing of the Pilgrims,* pages 94–100. Ask for an oral or written narration.

Grades 7–9: Read with your older children or assign as independent reading *Poor Richard,* chapter 14. Ask for an oral or written narration.

Grades 10–12: Read with your older children or assign as independent reading about 7 pages of *The Autobiography of Benjamin Franklin,* from the

two things he regretted through his not contesting a copy of his open stove invention. Ask for an oral or written narration.

Lesson 37: Georgia

Materials Needed
- *Stories of America, Volume 1*
- *The Landing of the Pilgrims* (grades 4–6)
- *Poor Richard* (grades 7–9)
- *The Autobiography of Benjamin Franklin* (grades 10–12)

General Oglethrope settles Georgia (1733)

Family: Ask students what they recall from last time's reading about the Carolinas. Look at the map on page 181 in *Stories of America, Volume 1*, and see what land area is left to learn about south of the Carolinas. Write "Georgia" and "Oglethorpe" on a sheet of paper or small whiteboard. Read together chapter 9, "Georgia," and ask for an oral narration.

Grades 4–6: Read with your older children or assign as independent reading *The Landing of the Pilgrims,* pages 101–105. Ask for an oral or written narration.

Grades 7–9: Read with your older children or assign as independent reading *Poor Richard,* chapter 15. Ask for an oral or written narration.

Grades 10–12: Read with your older children or assign as independent reading about 7 pages of *The Autobiography of Benjamin Franklin,* from his establishing an academy through his helping Rev. Gilbert Tennent erect a meeting-house. Ask for an oral or written narration.

Lesson 38: Preparing for the cape & Philippians 3 and 4

Materials Needed
- *Sailing Alone Around the World*
- Outline map of South America; labeled world map
- Bible
- *GOAL Bible Study Journal*
- *Discovering Doctrine* (grades 7–12)

Family Geography Book: Ask students what they recall about Joshua Slocum's trip from Gibraltar and his decided course. Read together *Sailing Alone Around the World,* the last half of chapter 5, and ask for an oral narration. See if students can trace on the world map from Boston to Nova Scotia to the Azores to Gibraltar to Pernambuco in South America.

*Book of Centuries
Timeline*

Family Map Drill: Give each student a copy of an outline map of South America. Encourage them to label all the countries that they know on the maps. Compare their labeled countries with a labeled world map and make any necessary corrections. Then have them label two or three more countries on their maps, copying the spelling and locations from the labeled world map.

Family Bible Study: Review your findings from last time then read together Philippians 3 and 4, looking for any descriptions of promises, commands, sins, or principles. Record your findings in your *GOAL Bible Study Journal.* Older students should also be listening for doctrinal truths that they can add to their ongoing *Discovering Doctrine* books.

Lesson 39: The Power Behind the Throne

Materials Needed
- *Stories of the Nations, Volume 1*
- (optional) *Master Skylark*
- *A Lion to Guard Us* (grades 1–3)
- *Along Came Galileo* (grades 4–6)
- *Famous Men of the 16th and 17th Century* (grades 7–12)

Richelieu, the power behind King Louis XIII (1585–1642)

Family: Ask students what they recall from last time's reading about Galileo. Read together *Stories of the Nations, Volume 1,* chapter 7, "The Power Behind the Throne." Locate France on the map on page 155, and ask for an oral narration.

Optional Family Read-Aloud: Read together *Master Skylark*, chapter 25, "The Waning of the Year."

Grades 1–3: Explain that the book you are about to read is based on a true story that happened at the same time as Shakespeare, Galileo, Kepler, and Richelieu. Read together *A Lion to Guard Us,* chapters 1–3.

Grades 4–6: Read with your older children or assign as independent reading *Along Came Galileo*, chapter 2, "Galileo's World." Ask for an oral or written narration.

Grades 7–12: Read with your older children or assign as independent reading *Famous Men of the 16th and 17th Century,* chapter 14, "Cardinal Richelieu." Ask for an oral or written narration.

Lesson 40: In Galileo's Day, part 1

Materials Needed
- (optional) *Master Skylark*

• *A Lion to Guard Us* (grades 1–3)
• *Along Came Galileo* (grades 4–6)
• *Famous Men of the 16th and 17th Century* (grades 7–12)

Optional Family Read-Aloud: Read together *Master Skylark*, chapters 26 and 27, "To Sing before the Queen" and "The Queen's Plaisance."

Grades 1–3: Read together *A Lion to Guard Us,* chapters 4–6.

Grades 4–6: Read with your older children or assign as independent reading *Along Came Galileo*, chapter 3, "Galileo Goes to College." Ask for an oral or written narration.

Grades 7–12: Read with your older children or assign as independent reading *Famous Men of the 16th and 17th Century*, chapter 15, "Charles I." Ask for an oral or written narration.

Tip: Make sure older children are up to date with their Book of Centuries entries.

 # Lesson 41: The Native Americans

Materials Needed
• *Stories of America, Volume 1*
• *Tapenum's Day* (grades 1–3)
• *The Landing of the Pilgrims* (grades 4–6)
• *Poor Richard* (grades 7–9)
• *The Autobiography of Benjamin Franklin* (grades 10–12)
• *American Voices* (grades 10–12)

Family: Ask students what they recall from last time's reading about Georgia. Read together *Stories of America, Volume 1*, chapter 10, "The Native Americans," and ask for an oral narration.

Read together the poem "Indian Names" from *Stories of America, Volume 1*, pages 63 and 64. Discuss any regions near where you live that have an Indian name.

Grades 1–3: Read together *Tapenum's Day.*

Grades 4–6: Read with your older children or assign as independent reading *The Landing of the Pilgrims*, pages 106–110. Ask for an oral or written narration.

Grades 7–9: Read with your older children or assign as independent reading *Poor Richard*, chapter 16. Ask for an oral or written narration.

Grades 10–12: Read with your older children or assign as independent reading about 7 pages of *The Autobiography of Benjamin Franklin,* from his improving the streets of Philadelphia through the House voting while he was absent. Ask for an oral or written narration.

King Philip's War (1675–1676)

Also read with your older children or assign as independent reading *American Voices,* pages 30 and 31, "Albany Plan of Union," and ask for a narration that outlines the chain of authority and the responsibilities of the Grand Council as Franklin proposed.

 # Lesson 42: Colonial Times, part 7

Materials Needed
- *The Courage of Sarah Noble* (grades 1–3)
- *The Landing of the Pilgrims* (grades 4–6)
- *Poor Richard* (grades 7–9)
- *The Autobiography of Benjamin Franklin* (grades 10–12)

Grades 1–3: Read together *The Courage of Sarah Noble,* chapter 1, "Night in the Forest."

Grades 4–6: Read with your older children or assign as independent reading *The Landing of the Pilgrims,* pages 111–117. Ask for an oral or written narration.

Grades 7–9: Read with your older children or assign as independent reading *Poor Richard,* chapter 17. Ask for an oral or written narration.

Grades 10–12: Read with your older children or assign as independent reading about 7 pages of *The Autobiography of Benjamin Franklin,* from his meeting Mr. Morris through his getting repaid by the general the day before the battle. Ask for an oral or written narration.

 # Lesson 43: Departure from Rio de Janeiro & Colossians 1 and 2

Materials Needed
- *Sailing Alone Around the World*
- Outline map of South America; labeled world map
- Bible
- *GOAL Bible Study Journal*
- *Discovering Doctrine* (grades 7–12)

Family Geography Book: Ask students what they recall about Joshua Slocum's time in Pernambuco. Read together *Sailing Alone Around the World,* the first half of chapter 6, and ask for an oral narration. See if students can trace on the world map from Boston to Nova Scotia to the Azores to Gibraltar to Pernambuco to Rio de Janeiro to Uruguay.

Family Map Drill: Give each student a copy of an outline map of South

America. Encourage them to label all the countries that they know on the maps. Compare their labeled countries with a labeled world map and make any necessary corrections. Then have them label two or three more countries on their maps, copying the spelling and locations from the labeled world map.

Family Bible Study: Review your findings from last time then read together Colossians 1 and 2, looking for any descriptions of promises, commands, sins, or principles. Record your findings in your *GOAL Bible Study Journal.* Older students should also be listening for doctrinal truths that they can add to their ongoing *Discovering Doctrine* books.

Lesson 44: In Galileo's Day, part 2

Materials Needed
- (optional) *Master Skylark*
- *A Lion to Guard Us* (grades 1–3)
- *Along Came Galileo* (grades 4–6)
- *Famous Men of the 16th and 17th Century* (grades 7–12)

Optional Family Read-Aloud: Read together *Master Skylark*, chapters 28 and 29, "Christmas with Queen Bess" and "Back to Gaston Carew."

Grades 1–3: Ask students to recall what has happened so far in the story. Read together *A Lion to Guard Us,* chapters 7–9.

Grades 4–6: Read with your older children or assign as independent reading *Along Came Galileo,* chapter 4, "Galileo Becomes a Professor." Ask for an oral or written narration.

Grades 7–12: Read with your older children or assign as independent reading *Famous Men of the 16th and 17th Century,* chapter 16, "Oliver Cromwell." Ask for an oral or written narration.

Lesson 45: In Galileo's Day, part 3

Materials Needed
- (optional) *Master Skylark*
- *A Lion to Guard Us* (grades 1–3)
- *Along Came Galileo* (grades 4–6)
- *Famous Men of the 16th and 17th Century* (grades 7–12)

Optional Family Read-Aloud: Read together *Master Skylark*, chapters 30 and 31, "At the Falcon Inn" and "In the Twinkling of an Eye."

Grades 1–3: Read together *A Lion to Guard Us,* chapters 10–12.

Grades 4–6: Read with your older children or assign as independent reading *Along Came Galileo*, chapter 5, "Three Famous Astronomers." Ask for an oral or written narration.

Grades 7–12: Read with your older children or assign as independent reading *Famous Men of the 16th and 17th Century,* chapter 17, "William Bradford." Ask for an oral or written narration.

Tip: Make sure older children are up to date with their Book of Centuries entries.

 # Lesson 46: Colonial Times, part 8

Materials Needed
- *The Courage of Sarah Noble* (grades 1–3)
- *The Landing of the Pilgrims* (grades 4–6)
- *Poor Richard* (grades 7–9)
- *The Autobiography of Benjamin Franklin* (grades 10–12)

Grades 1–3: Read together *The Courage of Sarah Noble,* chapter 2, "Night in the Settlement."

Grades 4–6: Read with your older children or assign as independent reading *The Landing of the Pilgrims,* pages 118–129. Ask for an oral or written narration.

Grades 7–9: Read with your older children or assign as independent reading *Poor Richard,* chapter 18. Ask for an oral or written narration.

Grades 10–12: Read with your older children or assign as independent reading about 7 pages of *The Autobiography of Benjamin Franklin,* from his description of the general through his scheme for encouraging the men to attend prayer services. Ask for an oral or written narration.

 # Lesson 47: Colonial Times, part 9

Materials Needed
- *The Courage of Sarah Noble* (grades 1–3)
- *The Landing of the Pilgrims* (grades 4–6)
- *Poor Richard* (grades 7–9)
- *The Autobiography of Benjamin Franklin* (grades 10–12)

Grades 1–3: Read together *The Courage of Sarah Noble,* chapter 3, "Down the Long Hill."

Grades 4–6: Read with your older children or assign as independent

reading *The Landing of the Pilgrims,* pages 130–138. Ask for an oral or written narration.

Grades 7–9: Read with your older children or assign as independent reading *Poor Richard,* chapter 19. Ask for an oral or written narration.

Grades 10–12: Read with your older children or assign as independent reading about 7 pages of *The Autobiography of Benjamin Franklin,* from his being called back to the Assembly through the Royal Society voting him a member. Ask for an oral or written narration.

Reminder: If you want to do a hands-on project for lesson 57, start collecting your resources now. See page 58 for details.

Lesson 48: An excursion to Buenos Aires & Colossians 3 and 4

Materials Needed
- *Sailing Alone Around the World*
- Outline map of South America; labeled world map
- Bible
- *GOAL Bible Study Journal*
- *Discovering Doctrine* (grades 7–12)

Family Geography Book: See if students can trace on the world map from Boston to Nova Scotia to the Azores to Gibraltar to Pernambuco to Rio de Janeiro to Uruguay. Ask students what they recall about Joshua Slocum's time in Uruguay. Read together *Sailing Alone Around the World*, the last half of chapter 6, and ask for an oral narration.

Family Map Drill: Give each student a copy of an outline map of South America. Encourage them to label all the countries that they know on the maps. Compare their labeled countries with a labeled world map and make any necessary corrections. Then have them label two or three more countries on their maps, copying the spelling and locations from the labeled world map.

Family Bible Study: Review your findings from last time then read together Colossians 3 and 4, looking for any descriptions of promises, commands, sins, or principles. Record your findings in your *GOAL Bible Study Journal*. Older students should also be listening for doctrinal truths that they can add to their ongoing *Discovering Doctrine* books.

Lesson 49: In Galileo's Day, part 4

Materials Needed
- (optional) *Master Skylark*

• *A Lion to Guard Us* (grades 1–3)
• *Along Came Galileo* (grades 4–6)
• *Famous Men of the 16th and 17th Century* (grades 7–12)

Optional Family Read-Aloud: Read together *Master Skylark*, chapters 32 and 33, "The Last of Gaston Carew" and "Cicely Disappears."

Grades 1–3: Ask students to recall what has happened so far in the story. Read together *A Lion to Guard Us,* chapters 13–15.

Grades 4–6: Read with your older children or assign as independent reading *Along Came Galileo*, chapter 6, "A New Way of Looking." Ask for an oral or written narration.

Grades 7–12: Read with your older children or assign as independent reading *Famous Men of the 16th and 17th Century*, chapter 18, "John Winthrop." Ask for an oral or written narration.

 # Lesson 50: In Galileo's Day, part 5

Materials Needed
• (optional) *Master Skylark*
• *A Lion to Guard Us* (grades 1–3)
• *Along Came Galileo* (grades 4–6)
• *Famous Men of the 16th and 17th Century* (grades 7–12)

Optional Family Read-Aloud: Read together *Master Skylark*, chapters 34 and 35, "The Bandy-legged Man" and "A Sudden Resolve."

Grades 1–3: Read together *A Lion to Guard Us,* chapters 16–18.

Grades 4–6: Read with your older children or assign as independent reading *Along Came Galileo*, chapter 7, "The Starry Messenger." Ask for an oral or written narration.

Grades 7–12: Read with your older children or assign as independent reading *Famous Men of the 16th and 17th Century*, chapter 19, "Blaise Pascal." Ask for an oral or written narration.

Reminder: Start gathering the resources you will need for Term 2. See page 61.

 # Lesson 51: Colonial Times, part 10

Materials Needed
• *The Courage of Sarah Noble* (grades 1–3)
• *The Landing of the Pilgrims* (grades 4–6)
• *Poor Richard* (grades 7–9)

• *The Autobiography of Benjamin Franklin* (grades 10–12)

Grades 1–3: Read together *The Courage of Sarah Noble,* chapter 4, "Night in the Cave."

Grades 4–6: Read with your older children or assign as independent reading *The Landing of the Pilgrims,* pages 139–144. Ask for an oral or written narration.

Grades 7–9: Read with your older children or assign as independent reading *Poor Richard,* chapter 20. Ask for an oral or written narration.

Grades 10–12: Read with your older children or assign as independent reading about 7 pages of *The Autobiography of Benjamin Franklin,* from the governor's presentation of the medal through his being detained in New York and not being paid. Ask for an oral or written narration.

 ## Lesson 52: Colonial Times, part 11

Materials Needed
• *The Courage of Sarah Noble* (grades 1–3)
• *The Landing of the Pilgrims* (grades 4–6)
• *Poor Richard* (if needed to catch up) (grades 7–9)
• *The Autobiography of Benjamin Franklin* (grades 10–12)

Grades 1–3: Read together *The Courage of Sarah Noble,* chapter 5, "Indians!" (Note: Students will finish *The Courage of Sarah Noble* next term.)

Grades 4–6: Read with your older children or assign as independent reading *The Landing of the Pilgrims,* pages 145–149. Ask for an oral or written narration. (Note: If students need more time to finish the book, they can catch up next week along with the exams.)

Grades 7–9: Use today to catch up on any reading and narration assignments from *Poor Richard.*

Grades 10–12: Read with your older children or assign as independent reading the rest of *The Autobiography of Benjamin Franklin,* from the captain's boast of a swift ship through the end of Part Four. Ask for an oral or written narration.

 ## Lesson 53: Weighing anchor at Buenos Aires & Philemon

Materials Needed
• *Sailing Alone Around the World*
• Outline map of South America; labeled world map

Book of Centuries Timeline

• Bible
• *GOAL Bible Study Journal*
• *Discovering Doctrine* (grades 7–12)

Family Geography Book: See if students can trace on the world map from Boston to Nova Scotia to the Azores to Gibraltar to Pernambuco to Rio de Janeiro to Uruguay to Buenos Aires. Ask students what they recall about Joshua Slocum's excursion to Buenos Aires. Read together *Sailing Alone Around the World*, the first half of chapter 7, and ask for an oral narration.

Tip: Make sure the students are tracing Slocum's trip on the world map as you read.

Family Map Drill: Give each student a copy of an outline map of South America. Encourage them to label all the countries that they know on the maps. Compare their labeled countries with a labeled world map and make any necessary corrections. Then have them label two or three more countries on their maps, copying the spelling and locations from the labeled world map.

Family Bible Study: Review your findings from last time then read together Philemon, looking for any descriptions of promises, commands, sins, or principles. Record your findings in your *GOAL Bible Study Journal*. Older students should also be listening for doctrinal truths that they can add to their ongoing *Discovering Doctrine* books.

Lesson 54: In Galileo's Day, part 6

Materials Needed
• (optional) *Master Skylark*
• *A Lion to Guard Us* (grades 1–3)
• *Along Came Galileo* (grades 4–6)
• *Famous Men of the 16th and 17th Century* (grades 7–12)

Optional Family Read-Aloud: Read together *Master Skylark*, chapters 36 and 37, "Wayfaring Home" and "Turned Adrift."

Grades 1–3: Ask students to recall what has happened so far in the story. Read together *A Lion to Guard Us,* chapters 19–21.

Grades 4–6: Read with your older children or assign as independent reading *Along Came Galileo*, chapters 8 and 9, "Galileo Loves a Fight" and "Trouble Begins." Ask for an oral or written narration.

Grades 7–12: Read with your older children or assign as independent reading *Famous Men of the 16th and 17th Century*, chapter 20, "Rembrandt." Ask for an oral or written narration.

Lesson 55: In Galileo's Day, part 7

Materials Needed
- (optional) *Master Skylark*
- *A Lion to Guard Us* (grades 1–3)
- *Along Came Galileo* (grades 4–6)
- *Famous Men of the 16th and 17th Century* (grades 7–12)

Optional Family Read-Aloud: Read together *Master Skylark*, chapters 38 and 39, "A Strange Day" and "All's Well that Ends Well."

Grades 1–3: Read together *A Lion to Guard Us,* chapters 22 and 23. Be sure to read the Historical Note too for a wonderful mental "connection" opportunity.

Grades 4–6: Read with your older children or assign as independent reading *Along Came Galileo*, chapters 10 and 11, "The Trial of Galileo" and "Galileo's Last Years." Ask for an oral or written narration.

Grades 7–12: Read with your older children or assign as independent reading *Famous Men of the 16th and 17th Century*, chapter 21, "John Milton." Ask for an oral or written narration.

Tip: Make sure older children are up to date with their Book of Centuries entries.

 # Lesson 56: American History Catch Up or Exam

Materials Needed
- *The Landing of the Pilgrims* (if doing catch-up reading) (grades 4–6)
- *The Autobiography of Benjamin Franklin* (if doing catch-up reading) (grades 10–12)

Family: Use today to catch up on any American History reading you need to finish, or use the questions below to begin the students' exam on Early American history.

Tip: Exams in a Charlotte Mason school require no "cramming" or preparation. You may be pleasantly surprised at what your students remember with no prompting.

Grades 1–3: Tell about a group of people who came to settle in America.
Grades 4–6: Select one of the following groups and tell all you remember about them from your readings so far: Puritans, Quakers, Catholics, Native Americans.
Grades 7–9: Select two of the following colonies and tell all you remember

about who settled there and why: Virginia, Rhode Island, Pennsylvania, Carolinas, Georgia.

Grades 10–12: Describe fully how the east coast of America was settled. Include the groups of people who came, their leaders, and their dealings with the Native Americans.

Tip: You may want to assign the older students to write their exam answers. Younger students may do oral exams; you might want to write or type their answers as they tell what they know. Or, if you have students in more than one grade level, you might allow them to do their exams orally in a group. That way the older can hear the younger, and the younger can hear the older.

 Lesson 57: American History Project or Exam

Materials Needed
- (optional) Materials for hands-on project

Family: Do a hands-on project (see below), or use the questions below to continue the students' exam on Early American history.

Grades 1–3: Tell what daily life was like for the Pilgrims as they lived in America.

Grades 4–6: Tell all you can remember about the Pilgrims.

Grades 7–9: Describe at least three of Benjamin Franklin's inventions and ideas for the public good.

Grades 10–12: Benjamin Franklin summarized his philosophy toward God and toward man in this quote from his autobiography:

> "That there is one God, who made all things.
> That he governs the world by his providence.
> That he ought to be worshipped by adoration, prayer, and thanksgiving.
> But that the most acceptable service of God is doing good to man.
> That the soul is immortal.
> And that God will certainly reward virtue and punish vice either here or hereafter."

Describe how this philosophy showed in Franklin's life, citing specific examples, and compare his philosophy to your own worldview.

Optional Hands-On Project: Select a Colonial America hands-on project from the Links and Tips page: http://SimplyCharlotteMason.com/books/early-modern/links-tips/

Lesson 58: Three Island Cove & Bible Exam

Materials Needed
- *Sailing Alone Around the World*
- Labeled world map

Family Geography Book: Ask students what they recall about Joshua Slocum's trip through the Strait of Magellan. See if students can trace on the world map from Boston to Nova Scotia to the Azores to Gibraltar to Pernambuco to Rio de Janeiro to Uruguay to Buenos Aires to the Strait of Magellan. Ask students what they recall about Joshua Slocum's excursion to Buenos Aires to the Strait of Magellan. Read together *Sailing Alone Around the World*, the last half of chapter 7, and ask for an oral narration.

Bible Exam: Use the questions below for the students' exam on Ephesians, Philippians, Colossians, and Philemon.

Grades 1–3: Name two GOAL items you have found in Ephesians, Philippians, Colossians, or Philemon and been able to do, not just hear.
Grades 4–12: Name the four things you are looking for in the Bible passages you have been reading (GOAL) and give at least one example of each from Ephesians, Philippians, Colossians, or Philemon.

Tip: If you assigned Scripture memory from Ephesians, Philippians, Colossians, and Philemon, you might also ask for a recitation of the passage(s). Be sure to encourage the children to say beautiful words in a beautiful way as they recite.

Lesson 59: World History Exam

Materials Needed
- *Famous Men of the 16th and 17th Century* (grades 7–12)

Family: Use the questions below to begin the students' exam on Early Modern world history.

Grades 1–3: Tell the story of a king or queen about whom you have read this term.
Grades 4–6: Tell all you know about England during the time of Queen Elizabeth.
Grades 7–9: Tell the stories of two of these English famous men: Sir Walter Raleigh, James I, John Smith, Oliver Cromwell, William Bradford.
Grades 10–12: How have you seen the truth of this line from Wordsworth, "the child is father to the man," in the various famous men about whom you have read? Mention at least four men, citing examples from their lives.

*Book of Centuries
Timeline*

Grades 7–12: Read with your older children or assign as independent reading *Famous Men of the 16th and 17th Century,* chapter 22, "Johannes Vermeer." Ask for an oral or written narration.

Lesson 60: World History Exam

Family: Use the questions below to continue the students' exam on Early Modern world history.

Grades 1–3: Tell the story of a famous man about whom you have read this term.

Grades 4–6: Tell all you know about Galileo.

Grades 7–9: Tell the stories of two of these famous Frenchmen: Henry of Navarre, Samuel de Champlain, Richelieu, Blaise Pascal.

Grades 10–12: Tell about the religious struggles during the 16th and 17th centuries. Explain how various rulers in different countries chose to deal with those struggles and the results that ensued, citing at least three examples from your reading.

Term 2

(12 weeks; 5 lessons/week)

American History Resources

- *Stories of America, Volume 1,* by Charles Morris and Sonya Shafer

Grades 1–3
- *The Courage of Sarah Noble* by Alice Dalgliesh
- *Toliver's Secret* by Esther Wood Brady

Grades 4–6
- *The Sign of the Beaver* by Elizabeth George Speare

Grades 7–9
- *Carry On, Mr. Bowditch* by Jean Lee Latham
- Book of Centuries (one for each student)

Grades 10–12
- *The Boys of '76* by Charles Coffin
- *American Voices* edited by Ray Notgrass
- Book of Centuries (one for each student)

Optional Resources
- Dover coloring books
    Heroes and Heroines of the American Revolution
    Story of the American Revolution
- Various resources for optional hands-on projects

World History, Bible, Geography Resources

- *Stories of the Nations, Volume 1,* by Charles Morris, Lorene Lambert, and Sonya Shafer
- *Jesus Is Better: Lessons from Hebrews* by Sonya Shafer
- Bible
- *Sailing Alone Around the World* by Joshua Slocum
- *Uncle Josh's Outline Map book or CD* by George and Hannah Wiggers (or other outline maps of South America and Australia)
- Labeled world map

Grades 1–3
- *Dangerous Journey* by Oliver Hunkin
- *Peter the Great* by Diane Stanley
- *Can't You Make Them Behave, King George?* by Jean Fritz

Grades 4–6
- *Strangers in the Land* by Louise A. Vernon
- *The Ocean of Truth: The Story of Sir Isaac Newton* by Joyce McPherson

Grades 7–9
- *Famous Men of the 16th and 17th Century* by Robert G. Shearer
- *Kidnapped* by Robert Louis Stevenson
- *The World of William Penn* by Genevieve Foster
- *Hearts and Hands: Chronicles of the Awakening Church* by Mindy and Brandon Withrow
- *Discovering Doctrine* by Sonya Shafer (one for each student)
- Book of Centuries (one for each student)

Grades 10–12
- *Famous Men of the 16th and 17th Century* by Robert G. Shearer
- *Waverley, Volume 1,* by Walter Scott
- *The World of William Penn* by Genevieve Foster
- *Hearts and Hands: Chronicles of the Awakening Church* by Mindy and Brandon Withrow
- "Sinners in the Hands of an Angry God" by Jonathan Edwards
- *Discovering Doctrine* by Sonya Shafer (one for each student)
- Book of Centuries (one for each student)

Optional Resources
- Dover coloring books
   French Baroque and Rococo Fashions

	Family	Grades 1–3	Grades 4–6	Grades 7–9	Grades 10–12
Week 1					
Bible	Hebrews Study, lesson 1				
World History	Stories of the Nations, Vol. 1, ch. 8, 9	Dangerous Journey, ch. 1	Strangers in the Land, ch. 1, 2	Famous Men of the 16th and 17th Century, ch. 23, 24; Kidnapped ch. 1, 2	Famous Men of the 16th and 17th Century, ch. 23, 24; Waverley, Vol. 1, ch. 1, 2
Geography	Sailing Alone Around the World, ch. 8; Map Drill: South America				
American History		Courage of Sarah Noble, ch. 6, 7 ✓	Sign of the Beaver, ch. 1, 2	Carry On, Mr. Bowditch, ch. 1, 2	The Boys of '76, ch. 1, 2
Week 2					
Bible	Hebrews Study, lesson 2				
World History		Dangerous Journey, ch. 2, 3	Strangers in the Land, ch. 3, 4	Famous Men of the 16th and 17th Century, ch. 25, 26; Kidnapped ch. 3, 4	Famous Men of the 16th and 17th Century, ch. 25, 26; Waverley, Vol. 1, ch. 3, 4
Geography	Sailing Alone Around the World, ch. 9A; Map Drill: South America				
American History		Courage of Sarah Noble, ch. 8, 9	Sign of the Beaver, ch. 3, 4	Carry On, Mr. Bowditch, ch. 3, 4	The Boys of '76, ch. 3, 4
Week 3					
Bible	Hebrews Study, lesson 3				
World History		Dangerous Journey, ch. 4, 5	Strangers in the Land, ch. 5, 6	Famous Men of the 16th and 17th Century, ch. 27, 28; Kidnapped ch. 5, 6	Famous Men of the 16th and 17th Century, ch. 27, 28; Waverley, Vol. 1, ch. 5, 6
Geography	Sailing Alone Around the World, ch. 9B; Map Drill: South America				
American History		Courage of Sarah Noble, ch. 10, 11	Sign of the Beaver, ch. 5, 6	Carry On, Mr. Bowditch, ch. 5, 6	The Boys of '76, ch. 5, 6
Week 4					
Bible	Hebrews Study, lesson 4				
World History		Dangerous Journey, ch. 6, 7	Strangers in the Land, ch. 7, 8	The World of William Penn, pp. 9–52; Kidnapped, ch. 7–9	The World of William Penn, pp. 9–52; Waverley, Vol. 1, ch. 7–10
Geography	Sailing Alone Around the World, ch. 10; Map Drill: South America				
American History	Stories of America, Vol. 1, ch. 11, 12 ●		Sign of the Beaver, ch. 7, 8	Carry On, Mr. Bowditch, ch. 7, 8	The Boys of '76, ch. 7, 8; American Voices, pp. 32–35

	Family	Grades 1–3	Grades 4–6	Grades 7–9	Grades 10–12
Week 5					
Bible	Hebrews Study, lesson 5				
World History		Dangerous Journey, ch. 8, 9	Strangers in the Land, ch. 9–11	The World of William Penn, parts 2, 3; Kidnapped, ch. 10–12	The World of William Penn, parts 2, 3; Waverley, Vol. 1, ch. 11–14
Geography	Sailing Alone Around the World, ch. 11A; Map Drill: South America				
American History	Stories of America, Vol. 1, ch. 13, 14		Sign of the Beaver, ch. 9, 10	Carry On, Mr. Bowditch, ch. 9, 10	The Boys of '76, ch. 9, 10
Week 6					
Bible	Hebrews Study, lesson 6				
World History	Stories of the Nations, Vol. 1, ch. 10, 11		Strangers in the Land, ch. 12; The Ocean of Truth, ch. 1	The World of William Penn, parts 4, 5; Kidnapped, ch. 13, 14	The World of William Penn, parts 4, 5; Waverley, Vol. 1, ch. 15, 16
Geography	Sailing Alone Around the World, ch. 11B; Map Drill: South America				
American History	Stories of America, Vol. 1, ch. 15, 16		Sign of the Beaver, ch. 11, 12	Carry On, Mr. Bowditch, ch. 11, 12	The Boys of '76, ch. 11, 12; American Voices, pp. 36–42
Week 7					
Bible	Hebrews Study, lesson 7				
World History	Stories of the Nations, Vol. 1, ch. 12	Peter the Great, pp. 4–19	The Ocean of Truth, ch. 2–5	The World of William Penn, parts 6, 7; Kidnapped, ch. 15–17	The World of William Penn, parts 6, 7; Waverley, Vol. 1, ch. 17–19
Geography	Sailing Alone Around the World, ch. 12A; Map Drill: Australia				
American History	Stories of America, Vol. 1, ch. 17, 18		Sign of the Beaver, ch. 13, 14	Carry On, Mr. Bowditch, ch. 13, 14	The Boys of '76, ch. 13, 14; American Voices, pp. 43–48
Week 8					
Bible	Hebrews Study, lesson 8				
World History		Peter the Great, pp. 20–32	The Ocean of Truth, ch. 6–9	The World of William Penn, parts 8, 9; Kidnapped, ch. 18–20	The World of William Penn, parts 8, 9; Waverley, Vol. 1, ch. 20–23
Geography	Sailing Alone Around the World, ch. 12B; Map Drill: Australia				
American History		Toliver's Secret, ch. 1, 2	Sign of the Beaver, ch. 15, 16	Carry On, Mr. Bowditch, ch. 15, 16	The Boys of '76, ch. 15, 16; American Voices, pp. 49–54

	Family	Grades 1–3	Grades 4–6	Grades 7–9	Grades 10–12
Week 9					
Bible	Hebrews Study, lesson 9				
World History	Stories of the Nations, Vol. 1, ch. 13 ,14	Can't You Make Them Behave, King George, pp. 6–15	The Ocean of Truth, ch. 10, 11	Hearts and Hands; Kidnapped, ch. 21, 22	Hearts and Hands; Sinners in the Hands of an Angry God; Waverley, Vol. 1, ch. 24
Geography	Sailing Alone Around the World, ch. 13A; Map Drill: Australia				
American History		Toliver's Secret, ch. 3, 4	Sign of the Beaver, ch. 17, 18	Carry On, Mr. Bowditch, ch. 17, 18	The Boys of '76, ch. 17, 18
Week 10					
Bible	Hebrews Study, lesson 10				
World History		Can't You Make Them Behave, King George, pp. 16–35	The Ocean of Truth, ch. 12–15	Hearts and Hands; Kidnapped, ch. 23–26	Hearts and Hands; Waverley, Vol. 1, ch. 25–28
Geography	Sailing Alone Around the World, ch. 13B; Map Drill: Australia				
American History		Toliver's Secret, ch. 5, 6	Sign of the Beaver, ch. 19, 20	Carry On, Mr. Bowditch, ch. 19, 20	The Boys of '76, ch. 19, 20
Week 11					
Bible	Hebrews Study, lesson 11				
World History	Stories of the Nations, Vol. 1, ch. 15	Can't You Make Them Behave, King George, pp. 36–46	The Ocean of Truth, ch. 16–Epilogue	Hearts and Hands; Kidnapped, ch. 27–30	Hearts and Hands; Waverley, Vol. 1, ch. 29–Author's Note
Geography	Sailing Alone Around the World, ch. 14A; Map Drill: Australia				
American History		Toliver's Secret, ch. 7, 8	Sign of the Beaver, ch. 21–23	Carry On, Mr. Bowditch, ch. 21, 22	The Boys of '76, ch. 21, 22
Week 12					
Bible	Exam				
World History	Exam				
Geography	Sailing Alone Around the World, ch. 14B				
American History	Exam		Sign of the Beaver, ch. 24, 25	Carry On, Mr. Bowditch, ch. 23, 24	

Lesson 61: Early America, part 1

Materials Needed
- *The Courage of Sarah Noble* (grades 1–3)
- *The Sign of the Beaver* (grades 4–6)
- *Carry On, Mr. Bowditch* (grades 7–9)
- *The Boys of '76* (grades 10–12)

Grades 1–3: Ask students what they recall about what has happened to Sarah Noble in past readings. Read together *The Courage of Sarah Noble,* chapter 6, "Friends."

Grades 4–6: Read with your older children or assign as independent reading *The Sign of the Beaver,* chapter 1. Ask for an oral or written narration if desired.

Grades 7–9: Read with your older children or assign as independent reading *Carry On, Mr. Bowditch,* chapter 1, "The Good-luck Spell." Ask for an oral or written narration if desired.

Grades 10–12: Read with your older children or assign as independent reading *The Boys of '76,* chapter 1, "The Alarm." Ask for an oral or written narration.

Tip: Grades 10–12 students will begin independent reading about the Revolutionary War now in order to allow them time to absorb this detailed account. The Family readings will catch up soon.

 # Lesson 62: Early America, part 2

Materials Needed
- *The Courage of Sarah Noble* (grades 1–3)
- *The Sign of the Beaver* (grades 4–6)
- *Carry On, Mr. Bowditch* (grades 7–9)
- *The Boys of '76* (grades 10–12)

Grades 1–3: Read together *The Courage of Sarah Noble,* chapter 7, "Keep up Your Courage."

Grades 4–6: Read with your older children or assign as independent reading *The Sign of the Beaver,* chapter 2. Ask for an oral or written narration if desired.

Grades 7–9: Read with your older children or assign as independent reading *Carry On, Mr. Bowditch,* chapter 2, "The Privateers." Ask for an oral or written narration if desired.

Grades 10–12: Read with your older children or assign as independent

reading *The Boys of '76,* chapter 2, "Bunker Hill." Ask for an oral or written narration.

 # Lesson 63: From Cape Pillar into the Pacific & Hebrews

Materials Needed
- *Sailing Alone Around the World*
- Outline map of South America; labeled world map
- Bible
- *Jesus Is Better: Lessons from Hebrews*

Family Geography Book: See if students can trace on the world map from Boston to Nova Scotia to the Azores to Gibraltar to Pernambuco to Rio de Janeiro to Uruguay to Buenos Aires to the Strait of Magellan. Ask students what they recall about Joshua Slocum's voyage so far. Read together *Sailing Alone Around the World,* chapter 8, and ask for an oral narration.

Tip: Don't forget to track Captain Slocum's voyage on a world map.

Family Map Drill: Give each student a copy of a blank outline map of South America. Encourage them to label all the countries that they know on the map. Compare their labeled countries with a labeled world map and make any necessary corrections. Then have them label two or three more countries on their maps, copying the spelling and locations from the labeled world map.

Family Bible Study: Complete *Jesus Is Better: Lessons from Hebrews,* lesson 1. Older students and adults may do the Additional Studies section, as well.

 # Lesson 64: The Dutch East India Company

Materials Needed
- *Stories of the Nations, Volume 1*
- *Strangers in the Land* (grades 4–6)
- *Famous Men of the 16th and 17th Century* (grades 7–12)
- *Kidnapped* (grades 7–9)
- *Waverley, Volume 1* (grades 10–12)

Family: Read together *Stories of the Nations, Volume 1,* chapter 8, "The Dutch East India Company." Trace the Dutch East India Company's locations using the maps on pages 155 and 165. Ask for an oral narration.

Dutch East India Company sets up spice monopoly (1602–1796)

Grades 4–6: Ask students what they recall about Richelieu and the Huguenots. Explain that this book is set in La Rochelle during that time. Read with your older children or assign as independent reading *Strangers in the Land,* chapter 1, "Midnight Meeting."

Grades 7–12: Read with your older children or assign as independent reading *Famous Men of the 16th and 17th Century,* chapter 23, "Charles II & James II." Ask for an oral or written narration.

Grades 7–9: Also assign as independent reading *Kidnapped,* chapter 1, "I Set Off upon My Journey to the House of Shaws."

Grades 10–12: Also assign as independent reading *Waverley, Volume 1,* chapter 1, "Introductory."

 Lesson 65: Kangxi, Emperor of China

Materials Needed
- *Stories of the Nations, Volume 1*
- *Dangerous Journey* (grades 1–3)
- *Strangers in the Land* (grades 4–6)
- *Famous Men of the 16th and 17th Century* (grades 7–12)
- *Kidnapped* (grades 7–9)
- *Waverley, Volume 1* (grades 10–12)

Family: Ask students what they recall from last time's reading about the Dutch East India Company. Write "Kangxi" on a small whiteboard or sheet of paper. Explain that today you will read a story about what was happening in China while the Dutch East India Company was selling spices. Read together *Stories of the Nations, Volume 1,* chapter 9, "Kangxi, Emperor of China." Use the map on page 165 to locate China. Ask for an oral narration.

Grades 1–3: Ask students what they recall hearing about religion so far in their readings. Explain that the book they are about to read was written by a man who lived in England at the same time as the Dutch East India Company and Kangxi, and he was put into prison for preaching God's Word without permission from the king. John Bunyan wrote this story as a picture of the Christian life. Read together *Dangerous Journey,* chapter 1, "The Slough of Despond."

Grades 4–6: Read with your older children or assign as independent reading *Strangers in the Land,* chapter 2, "A Promise Not Kept."

Grades 7–12: Read with your older children or assign as independent reading *Famous Men of the 16th and 17th Century,* chapter 24, "Jan Sobieski." Ask for an oral or written narration.

Grades 7–9: Also assign as independent reading *Kidnapped,* chapter 2, "I Come to My Journey's End."

*Kangxi, emperor of China
(1661–1722)*

Grades 10–12: Also assign as independent reading *Waverley, Volume 1,* chapter 2, "Waverley Honour—A Retrospect."

Tip: Make sure older children are up to date with their Book of Centuries entries.

 # Lesson 66: Early America, part 3

Materials Needed
- *The Courage of Sarah Noble* (grades 1–3)
- *The Sign of the Beaver* (grades 4–6)
- *Carry On, Mr. Bowditch* (grades 7–9)
- *The Boys of '76* (grades 10–12)

Grades 1–3: Read together *The Courage of Sarah Noble,* chapter 8, "In the Indian House."

Grades 4–6: Read with your older children or assign as independent reading *The Sign of the Beaver,* chapter 3. Ask for an oral or written narration if desired.

Grades 7–9: Read with your older children or assign as independent reading *Carry On, Mr. Bowditch,* chapter 3, "Word from the Pilgrim." Ask for an oral or written narration if desired.

Grades 10–12: Read with your older children or assign as independent reading *The Boys of '76,* chapter 3, "Battle of Bunker Hill." Ask for an oral or written narration.

 # Lesson 67: Early America, part 4

Materials Needed
- *The Courage of Sarah Noble* (grades 1–3)
- *The Sign of the Beaver* (grades 4–6)
- *Carry On, Mr. Bowditch* (grades 7–9)
- *The Boys of '76* (grades 10–12)

Grades 1–3: Read together *The Courage of Sarah Noble,* chapter 9, "Night of Fear."

Grades 4–6: Read with your older children or assign as independent reading *The Sign of the Beaver,* chapter 4. Ask for an oral or written narration if desired.

Grades 7–9: Read with your older children or assign as independent

reading *Carry On, Mr. Bowditch,* chapter 4, "Boys Don't Blubber." Ask for an oral or written narration if desired.

Grades 10–12: Read with your older children or assign as independent reading *The Boys of '76,* chapter 4, "Driving the British out of Boston." Ask for an oral or written narration.

Lesson 68: Savages and a spider-fight & Hebrews

Materials Needed
- *Sailing Alone Around the World*
- Outline map of South America; labeled world map
- Bible
- *Jesus Is Better: Lessons from Hebrews*

Family Geography Book: Ask students what they recall about Joshua Slocum's adventures near Cape Horn and the Strait of Magellan. Read together *Sailing Alone Around the World,* the first half of chapter 9, and ask for an oral narration. See if students can trace on the world map from Boston to Nova Scotia to the Azores to Gibraltar to Pernambuco to Rio de Janeiro to Uruguay to Buenos Aires to the Strait of Magellan. Make sure students know where Cape Horn is too.

Family Map Drill: Give each student a copy of an outline map of South America. Encourage them to label all the countries that they know on the map. Compare their labeled countries with a labeled world map and make any necessary corrections. Then have them label two or three more countries on their maps, copying the spelling and locations from the labeled world map.

Family Bible Study: Complete *Jesus Is Better: Lessons from Hebrews,* lesson 2. Older students and adults may do the Additional Studies section, as well.

 # Lesson 69: Late 1600s, part 1

Materials Needed
- *Dangerous Journey* (grades 1–3)
- *Strangers in the Land* (grades 4–6)
- *Famous Men of the 16th and 17th Century* (grades 7–12)
- *Kidnapped* (grades 7–9)
- *Waverley, Volume 1* (grades 10–12)

Grades 1–3: Ask students what they recall about what has happened so far to Pilgrim. Read together *Dangerous Journey,* chapter 2, "The Interpreter's House."

Grades 4–6: Read with your older children or assign as independent reading *Strangers in the Land,* chapter 3, "Threat to Freedom."

Grades 7–12: Read with your older children or assign as independent reading *Famous Men of the 16th and 17th Century,* chapter 25, "William of Orange." Ask for an oral or written narration.

Grades 7–9: Also assign as independent reading *Kidnapped,* chapter 3, "I Make Acquaintance of My Uncle."

Grades 10–12: Also assign as independent reading *Waverley, Volume 1,* chapter 3, "Education."

Reminder: Get the book The World of William Penn *for grades 7–12 for lesson 79.*

 # Lesson 70: Late 1600s, part 2

Materials Needed
- *Dangerous Journey* (grades 1–3)
- *Strangers in the Land* (grades 4–6)
- *Famous Men of the 16th and 17th Century* (grades 7–12)
- *Kidnapped* (grades 7–9)
- *Waverley, Volume 1* (grades 10–12)

Grades 1–3: Read together *Dangerous Journey,* chapter 3, "The Hill Difficulty."

Grades 4–6: Read with your older children or assign as independent reading *Strangers in the Land,* chapter 4, "Unfriendly Visitors."

Grades 7–12: Read with your older children or assign as independent reading *Famous Men of the 16th and 17th Century,* chapter 26, "John Locke." Ask for an oral or written narration.

Grades 7–9: Also assign as independent reading *Kidnapped,* chapter 4, "I Run a Great Danger in the House of Shaws."

Grades 10–12: Also assign as independent reading *Waverley, Volume 1,* chapter 4, "Castle-Building."

Tip: Make sure older children are up to date with their Book of Centuries entries.

 # Lesson 71: Early America, part 5

Materials Needed
- *The Courage of Sarah Noble* (grades 1–3)

- *The Sign of the Beaver* (grades 4–6)
- *Carry On, Mr. Bowditch* (grades 7–9)
- *The Boys of '76* (grades 10–12)

Grades 1–3: Read together *The Courage of Sarah Noble,* chapter 10, "Sarah goes Home."

Grades 4–6: Read with your older children or assign as independent reading *The Sign of the Beaver,* chapter 5. Ask for an oral or written narration if desired.

Grades 7–9: Read with your older children or assign as independent reading *Carry On, Mr. Bowditch,* chapter 5, "A Voice in the Night." Ask for an oral or written narration if desired.

Grades 10–12: Read with your older children or assign as independent reading *The Boys of '76,* chapter 5, "Expedition to Quebec." Ask for an oral or written narration.

 # Lesson 72: Early America, part 6

Materials Needed
- *The Courage of Sarah Noble* (grades 1–3)
- *The Sign of the Beaver* (grades 4–6)
- *Carry On, Mr. Bowditch* (grades 7–9)
- *The Boys of '76* (grades 10–12)

Grades 1–3: Read together *The Courage of Sarah Noble,* chapter 11, "Night in the Log House."

Grades 4–6: Read with your older children or assign as independent reading *The Sign of the Beaver,* chapter 6. Ask for an oral or written narration if desired.

Grades 7–9: Read with your older children or assign as independent reading *Carry On, Mr. Bowditch,* chapter 6, "Sail by Ash Breeze!" Ask for an oral or written narration if desired.

Grades 10–12: Read with your older children or assign as independent reading *The Boys of '76,* chapter 6, "Fort Sullivan." Ask for an oral or written narration.

 # Lesson 73: A chance cargo of tallow & Hebrews

Materials Needed
- *Sailing Alone Around the World*

Book of Centuries Timeline

- Outline map of South America; labeled world map
- Bible
- *Jesus Is Better: Lessons from Hebrews*

Family Geography Book: See if students can trace on the world map from Boston to Nova Scotia to the Azores to Gibraltar to Pernambuco to Rio de Janeiro to Uruguay to Buenos Aires through the Strait of Magellan. Ask students what they recall about Joshua Slocum's time back in the Strait's channels. Read together *Sailing Alone Around the World*, the last half of chapter 9, and ask for an oral narration.

Family Map Drill: Give each student a copy of an outline map of South America. Encourage them to label all the countries that they know on the map. Compare their labeled countries with a labeled world map and make any necessary corrections. Then have them label two or three more countries on their maps, copying the spelling and locations from the labeled world map.

Family Bible Study: Complete *Jesus Is Better: Lessons from Hebrews*, lesson 3. Older students and adults may do the Additional Studies section, as well.

Lesson 74: Late 1600s, part 3

Materials Needed
- *Dangerous Journey* (grades 1–3)
- *Strangers in the Land* (grades 4–6)
- *Famous Men of the 16th and 17th Century* (grades 7–12)
- *Kidnapped* (grades 7–9)
- *Waverley, Volume 1* (grades 10–12)

Grades 1–3: Ask students what they recall about what has happened so far to Pilgrim. Read together *Dangerous Journey*, chapter 4, "The Fight with Apollyon."

Grades 4–6: Read with your older children or assign as independent reading *Strangers in the Land*, chapter 5, "Conversion by Force."

Grades 7–12: Read with your older children or assign as independent reading *Famous Men of the 16th and 17th Century*, chapter 27, "Johan Pachelbel." Ask for an oral or written narration.

Grades 7–9: Also assign as independent reading *Kidnapped*, chapter 5, "I Go to the Queen's Ferry."

Grades 10–12: Also assign as independent reading *Waverley, Volume 1*, chapter 5, "Choice of a Profession."

Lesson 75: Late 1600s, part 4

Materials Needed
- *Dangerous Journey* (grades 1–3)

- *Strangers in the Land* (grades 4–6)
- *Famous Men of the 16th and 17th Century* (grades 7–12)
- *Kidnapped* (grades 7–9)
- *Waverley, Volume 1* (grades 10–12)

Grades 1–3: Read together *Dangerous Journey*, chapter 5, "The Valley of the Shadow of Death."

Tip: One of the illustrations in this chapter may be disturbing to a sensitive child, so display the pictures at your discretion.

Grades 4–6: Read with your older children or assign as independent reading *Strangers in the Land,* chapter 6, "A Child for the Church."

Grades 7–12: Read with your older children or assign as independent reading *Famous Men of the 16th and 17th Century,* chapter 28, "Louis XIV." Ask for an oral or written narration.

Grades 7–9: Also assign as independent reading *Kidnapped*, chapter 6, "What Befell at the Queen's Ferry."

Grades 10–12: Also assign as independent reading *Waverley, Volume 1,* chapter 6, "The Adieus of Waverley."

Tip: Make sure older children are up to date with their Book of Centuries entries.

Lesson 76: Royal Governors and Loyal Captains

Materials Needed
- *Stories of America, Volume 1*
- *The Sign of the Beaver* (grades 4–6)
- *Carry On, Mr. Bowditch* (grades 7–9)
- *The Boys of '76* (grades 10–12)
- *American Voices* (grades 10–12)

Family: Explain that when the settlers came over to America, they needed permission from their kings, for the kings thought they owned this land, though they had never seen it. Write the word "charter" on a sheet of paper or whiteboard. Read together *Stories of America, Volume 1*, chapter 11, "Royal Governors and Loyal Captains." Ask for an oral narration.

Grades 4–6: Read with your older children or assign as independent reading *The Sign of the Beaver,* chapter 7. Ask for an oral or written narration if desired.

Grades 7–9: Read with your older children or assign as independent

reading *Carry On, Mr. Bowditch,* chapter 7, "The Almanac." Ask for an oral or written narration if desired.

Grades 10–12: Read with your older children or assign as independent reading *The Boys of '76,* chapter 7, "Battle of Long Island." Ask for an oral or written narration.

Also read with your older children or assign as independent reading *American Voices,* pages 32 and 33, "Letters from a Farmer in Pennsylvania," and ask for a narration.

 # Lesson 77: Old Times in the Colonies

Materials Needed
- *Stories of America, Volume 1*
- *The Sign of the Beaver* (grades 4–6)
- *Carry On, Mr. Bowditch* (grades 7–9)
- *The Boys of '76* (grades 10–12)
- *American Voices* (grades 10–12)

Family: Ask students what they recall from the previous reading about Governors and Captains and Charters. Ask students if they have heard anything in their studies thus far that might give them some clues about what it would be like to live in Colonial America. Read together *Stories of America, Volume 1,* chapter 12, "Old Times in the Colonies." Ask for an oral or drawn narration. If students draw their narrations, ask them to tell you about their pictures.

Grades 4–6: Read with your older children or assign as independent reading *The Sign of the Beaver,* chapter 8. Ask for an oral or written narration if desired.

Grades 7–9: Read with your older children or assign as independent reading *Carry On, Mr. Bowditch,* chapter 8, "Lock, Stock, and Bookkeeper." Ask for an oral or written narration if desired.

Grades 10–12: Read with your older children or assign as independent reading *The Boys of '76,* chapter 8, "Evacuation of New York." Ask for an oral or written narration.

Also read with your older children or assign as independent reading *American Voices,* pages 34 and 35, "Poems by Phillis Wheatley."

 # Lesson 78: At Robinson Crusoe's anchorage & Hebrews

Materials Needed
- *Sailing Alone Around the World*

• Outline map of South America; labeled world map
• Bible
• *Jesus Is Better: Lessons from Hebrews*

Family Geography Book: Ask students what they recall about Captain Slocum's encounter with the canoes and his cargo of tallow. Read together *Sailing Alone Around the World*, chapter 10, and ask for an oral narration.

Family Map Drill: Give each student a copy of an outline map of South America. Add Central America too, if your outline map doesn't include those countries. Encourage them to label all the countries that they know on the map. Compare their labeled countries with a labeled world map and make any necessary corrections. Then have them label two or three more countries on their maps, copying the spelling and locations from the labeled world map.

Family Bible Study: Complete *Jesus Is Better: Lessons from Hebrews*, lesson 4. Older students and adults may do the Additional Studies section, as well.

Lesson 79: Late 1600s, part 5

Materials Needed
• *Dangerous Journey* (grades 1–3)
• *Strangers in the Land* (grades 4–6)
• *The World of William Penn* (grades 7–12)
• *Kidnapped* (grades 7–9)
• *Waverley, Volume 1* (grades 10–12)

Grades 1–3: Ask students what they recall about what has happened so far to Pilgrim. Read together *Dangerous Journey*, chapter 6, "Vanity Fair."

Tip: Use your discretion with the illustrations in this chapter also.

Grades 4–6: Read with your older children or assign as independent reading *Strangers in the Land,* chapter 7, "Secret Message."

Grades 7–12: Read with your older children or assign as independent reading *The World of William Penn,* part 1, "The Life Story of William Penn," pages 9–30. Ask for an oral or written narration.

Grades 7–9: Also assign as independent reading *Kidnapped*, chapters 7 and 8, "I Go to Sea in the Brig Covenant of Dysart" and "The Round-House."

Grades 10–12: Also assign as independent reading *Waverley, Volume 1,* chapters 7 and 8, "A Horse-Quarter in Scotland" and "A Scottish Manor-House Sixty Years Since."

Book of Centuries
Timeline

 # Lesson 80: Late 1600s, part 6

Materials Needed
- *Dangerous Journey* (grades 1–3)
- *Strangers in the Land* (grades 4–6)
- *The World of William Penn* (grades 7–12)
- *Kidnapped* (grades 7–9)
- *Waverley, Volume 1* (grades 10–12)

Grades 1–3: Read together *Dangerous Journey*, chapter 7, "Doubting Castle."

Grades 4–6: Read with your older children or assign as independent reading *Strangers in the Land,* chapter 8, "Trial for the Innocent."

Grades 7–12: Read with your older children or assign as independent reading *The World of William Penn*, part 1, "The Life Story of William Penn," pages 31–52. Ask for an oral or written narration.

Grades 7–9: Also assign as independent reading *Kidnapped*, chapter 9, "The Man with the Belt of Gold."

Grades 10–12: Also assign as independent reading *Waverley, Volume 1,* chapters 9 and 10, "More of the Manor-House and Its Environs" and "Rose Bradwardine and her Father."

Reminder: Get the book The Ocean of Truth *for grades 4–6 for lesson 90.*

Tip: Make sure older children are up to date with their Book of Centuries entries.

 # Lesson 81: Daniel Boone

Materials Needed
- *Stories of America, Volume 1*
- *The Sign of the Beaver* (grades 4–6)
- *Carry On, Mr. Bowditch* (grades 7–9)
- *The Boys of '76* (grades 10–12)

Family: Ask students what they recall from the previous reading about life in the colonies. Explain that we know about some famous colonists, who became famous for different reasons. Write "Daniel Boone" on a sheet of paper or whiteboard. Explain that today's reading is about a colonist who became famous as a hunter and tracker. Read together *Stories of America, Volume 1*, chapter 13, "Daniel Boone." Ask for an oral narration.

Grades 4–6: Read with your older children or assign as independent reading *The Sign of the Beaver,* chapter 9. Ask for an oral or written narration if desired.

Daniel Boone (1734–1820)

Grades 7–9: Read with your older children or assign as independent reading *Carry On, Mr. Bowditch,* chapter 9, "Anchor to Windward." Ask for an oral or written narration if desired.

Grades 10–12: Read with your older children or assign as independent reading *The Boys of '76,* chapter 9, "Battle of White Plains." Ask for an oral or written narration.

 ## Lesson 82: A Hero of the Colonies

Materials Needed
- *Stories of America, Volume 1*
- *The Sign of the Beaver* (grades 4–6)
- *Carry On, Mr. Bowditch* (grades 7–9)
- *The Boys of '76* (grades 10–12)

Family: Ask students what they recall from the previous reading about Daniel Boone. Explain that today's reading is about a colonist who became famous as a tracker, but also as a leader among soldiers. Read together *Stories of America, Volume 1*, chapter 14, "A Hero of the Colonies." Ask for an oral narration.

George Washington (1732–1799)

Grades 4–6: Read with your older children or assign as independent reading *The Sign of the Beaver,* chapter 10. Ask for an oral or written narration if desired.

Grades 7–9: Read with your older children or assign as independent reading *Carry On, Mr. Bowditch,* chapter 10, "Freedom." Ask for an oral or written narration if desired.

Grades 10–12: Read with your older children or assign as independent reading *The Boys of '76,* chapter 10, "Lake Champlain." Ask for an oral or written narration.

Lesson 83: Robinson Crusoe's realm & Hebrews

Materials Needed
- *Sailing Alone Around the World*
- Outline map of South America; labeled world map
- Bible
- *Jesus Is Better: Lessons from Hebrews*

Family Geography Book: See if students can trace on the world map from Boston to Nova Scotia to the Azores to Gibraltar to Pernambuco to Rio de Janeiro to Uruguay to Buenos Aires through the Strait of Magellan to Juan

Fernandez islands (west of Santiago, Chile). Ask students what they recall about Joshua Slocum's trip to Robinson Crusoe's island. Read together *Sailing Alone Around the World,* the first half of chapter 11, and ask for an oral narration.

Family Map Drill: Give each student a copy of an outline map of South America. Encourage them to label all the countries that they know on the map. Compare their labeled countries with a labeled world map and make any necessary corrections. Then have them label two or three more countries on their maps, copying the spelling and locations from the labeled world map.

> *Reminder: Make sure you have outline maps of Australia for lesson 93.*

Family Bible Study: Complete *Jesus Is Better: Lessons from Hebrews,* lesson 5. Older students and adults may do the Additional Studies section, as well.

 # Lesson 84: Late 1600s, part 7

Materials Needed
- *Dangerous Journey* (grades 1–3)
- *Strangers in the Land* (grades 4–6)
- *The World of William Penn* (grades 7–12)
- *Kidnapped* (grades 7–9)
- *Waverley, Volume 1* (grades 10–12)

Grades 1–3: Ask students what they recall about what has happened so far to Pilgrim. Read together *Dangerous Journey,* chapter 8, "The Dark River."

Grades 4–6: Read with your older children or assign as independent reading *Strangers in the Land,* chapter 9, "Three Days to Flee."

Grades 7–12: Read with your older children or assign as independent reading *The World of William Penn,* part 2, "Introducing Three French Explorers." Ask for an oral or written narration.

Grades 7–9: Also assign as independent reading *Kidnapped,* chapters 10 and 11, "The Siege of the Round-House" and "The Captain Knuckles Under."

Grades 10–12: Also assign as independent reading *Waverley, Volume 1,* chapters 11 and 12, "The Banquet" and "Repentance and a Reconciliation."

> *Reminder: Get the book* Peter the Great *for grades 1–3 for lesson 94.*

 # Lesson 85: Late 1600s, part 8

Materials Needed
- *Dangerous Journey* (grades 1–3)

• *Strangers in the Land* (grades 4–6)
• *The World of William Penn* (grades 7–12)
• *Kidnapped* (grades 7–9)
• *Waverley, Volume 1* (grades 10–12)

Grades 1–3: Read together *Dangerous Journey*, chapter 9, "Christiana's Story."

Grades 4–6: Read with your older children or assign as independent reading *Strangers in the Land,* chapters 10 and 11, "Trying to Escape" and "Surprise Voyage."

Grades 7–12: Read with your older children or assign as independent reading *The World of William Penn*, part 3, "Introducing Louis XIV." Ask for an oral or written narration.

Grades 7–9: Also assign as independent reading *Kidnapped*, chapter 12, "I Hear of the Red Fox."

Grades 10–12: Also assign as independent reading *Waverley, Volume 1*, chapters 13 and 14, "A More Rational Day Than the Last" and "Waverley Becomes Domesticated at Tully-Veolan."

Tip: Make sure older children are up to date with their Book of Centuries entries.

 # Lesson 86: The French and Indian War

Materials Needed
• *Stories of America, Volume 1*
• *The Sign of the Beaver* (grades 4–6)
• *Carry On, Mr. Bowditch* (grades 7–9)
• *The Boys of '76* (grades 10–12)

Family: Ask students what they recall from the previous reading about George Washington. Explain that the countries who had sent settlers over to America would often squabble over land and fights would break out between their settlers over here. Today's reading is about one such struggle that escalated into a war. Locate Nova Scotia on the map on page 181 in *Stories of America, Volume 1*, then read together chapter 15, "The French and Indian War." Ask for an oral narration.

Grades 4–6: Read with your older children or assign as independent reading *The Sign of the Beaver,* chapter 11. Ask for an oral or written narration if desired.

Grades 7–9: Read with your older children or assign as independent reading *Carry On, Mr. Bowditch,* chapter 11, "What Next?" Ask for an oral or written narration if desired.

*French and Indian War
(1754–1763)*

Grades 10–12: Read with your older children or assign as independent reading *The Boys of '76,* chapter 11, "Battle of Trenton." Ask for an oral or written narration.

Reminder: Get the book Toliver's Secret *for grades 1–3 for lesson 96.*

 # Lesson 87: Causes of the Revolution

Materials Needed
- *Stories of America, Volume 1*
- *The Sign of the Beaver* (grades 4–6)
- *Carry On, Mr. Bowditch* (grades 7–9)
- *The Boys of '76* (grades 10–12)
- *American Voices* (grades 10–12)

Albany Convention (1754)

Stamp Act (1765)

Boston Tea Party (1773)

Family: Ask students what they recall from the previous reading about the French and Indian War. Explain that sometimes there were struggles between the settlers and their own countries. Read together *Stories of America, Volume 1,* chapter 16, "Causes of the Revolution." Ask for an oral narration.

Grades 4–6: Read with your older children or assign as independent reading *The Sign of the Beaver,* chapter 12. Ask for an oral or written narration if desired.

Grades 7–9: Read with your older children or assign as independent reading *Carry On, Mr. Bowditch,* chapter 12, "Down to the Sea." Ask for an oral or written narration if desired.

Grades 10–12: Read with your older children or assign as independent reading *The Boys of '76,* chapter 12, "Princeton." Ask for an oral or written narration.

Also read with your older children or assign as independent reading *American Voices,* pages 36–42, "Give Me Liberty or Give Me Death" and "Common Sense (excerpts)," and ask for a narration.

 # Lesson 88: Sighting the Marquesas & Hebrews

Materials Needed
- *Sailing Alone Around the World*
- Outline map of South America; labeled world map
- Bible
- *Jesus Is Better: Lessons from Hebrews*

Family Geography Book: Ask students what they recall about Slocum's experiences on the island of Robinson Crusoe. Read together *Sailing Alone Around the World*, the last half of chapter 11, and ask for an oral narration. See if students can trace on the world map from Boston to Nova Scotia to the Azores to Gibraltar to Pernambuco to Rio de Janeiro to Uruguay to Buenos Aires to the Strait of Magellan to Juan Fernandez islands to the Marquesas islands (in French Polynesia).

Tip: If you have trouble locating some of the islands where Slocum landed, try using online mapping software to search for them.

Family Map Drill: Give each student a copy of an outline map of South America. Encourage them to label all the countries that they know on the map. Compare their labeled countries with a labeled world map and make any necessary corrections. Then have them label two or three more countries on their maps, copying the spelling and locations from the labeled world map.

Family Bible Study: Complete *Jesus Is Better: Lessons from Hebrews*, lesson 6. Older students and adults may do the Additional Studies section, as well.

Lesson 89: Two French Explorers in the New World

Materials Needed
- *Stories of the Nations, Volume 1*
- *Strangers in the Land* (grades 4–6)
- *The World of William Penn* (grades 7–12)
- *Kidnapped* (grades 7–9)
- *Waverley, Volume 1* (grades 10–12)

Marquette and Joliet explore the Mississippi River (1673)

Family: Ask students what they recall about the Old World and the New World. (The difference was explained in chapter 1.) Read together *Stories of the Nations, Volume 1*, chapter 10, "Two French Explorers in the New World." Use the map on page 159 to see which countries had settled in which areas of the world. (The map pictures the world territories at a later date than today's study, but it will give students an idea of where various countries settled.) Ask for an oral narration.

Grades 4–6: Read with your older children or assign as independent reading *Strangers in the Land*, chapter 12, "Strangers No Longer."

Grades 7–12: Read with your older children or assign as independent reading *The World of William Penn*, part 4, "Introducing Two Mogul Emperors of India." Ask for an oral or written narration.

Grades 7–9: Also assign as independent reading *Kidnapped*, chapter 13, "The Loss of the Brig."

Book of Centuries Timeline

 # Lesson 90: Isaac Newton and His Questions

Materials Needed

- *Stories of the Nations, Volume 1*
- *The Ocean of Truth* (grades 4–6)
- *The World of William Penn* (grades 7–12)
- *Kidnapped* (grades 7–9)
- *Waverley, Volume 1* (grades 10–12)

Family: Ask students what they recall from last time's reading about Marquette and Joliet. Write "Isaac Newton" on a whiteboard or sheet of paper. Read together *Stories of the Nations, Volume 1,* chapter 11, "Isaac Newton and His Questions." Ask for an oral narration.

Grades 4–6: Read with your older children or assign as independent reading *The Ocean of Truth,* chapter 1, "Telescopes and Tarts." Ask for an oral or written narration.

Grades 7–12: Read with your older children or assign as independent reading *The World of William Penn,* part 5, "Introducing Sir Isaac Newton." Ask for an oral or written narration.

Grades 7–9: Also assign as independent reading *Kidnapped,* chapter 14, "The Islet."

Grades 10–12: Also assign as independent reading *Waverley, Volume 1,* chapter 16, "An Unexpected Ally Appears."

Tip: Make sure older children are up to date with their Book of Centuries entries.

Isaac Newton learns about gravity (1643–1727)

Lesson 91: The Shot Heard 'Round the World

Materials Needed

- *Stories of America, Volume 1*
- *The Sign of the Beaver* (grades 4–6)
- *Carry On, Mr. Bowditch* (grades 7–9)
- *The Boys of '76* (grades 10–12)
- *American Voices* (grades 10–12)

Family: Ask students what they recall from the previous reading about the causes of the Revolution. Explain that these struggles banded the colonies together. Read together *Stories of America, Volume 1*, chapter 17, "The Shot Heard 'Round the World." Ask for an oral narration.

Explain that one man took the story of Paul Revere's warning the colonists and made it into a poem. Read together "Paul Revere's Ride" from *Stories of America, Volume 1*, pages 105–109.

Grades 4–6: Read with your older children or assign as independent reading *The Sign of the Beaver*, chapter 13. Ask for an oral or written narration if desired.

Grades 7–9: Read with your older children or assign as independent reading *Carry On, Mr. Bowditch*, chapter 13, "Discovery." Ask for an oral or written narration if desired.

Grades 10–12: Read with your older children or assign as independent reading *The Boys of '76*, chapter 13, "Ticonderoga and Hubbardton." Ask for an oral or written narration.

Also read with your older children or assign as independent reading *American Voices*, pages 43–46, "Declaration of Independence," and ask for a narration.

Lesson 92: Fighting for Freedom

Materials Needed
- *Stories of America, Volume 1*
- *The Sign of the Beaver* (grades 4–6)
- *Carry On, Mr. Bowditch* (grades 7–9)
- *The Boys of '76* (grades 10–12)
- *American Voices* (grades 10–12)

Family: Ask students what they recall from the previous reading about the shot heard 'round the world. Explain that a poet named Emerson wrote a poem about the battle at Concord. Read together "Concord Hymn" from *Stories of America, Volume 1*, page 111.

Explain that that battle was the beginning of a long war. Read together *Stories of America, Volume 1*, chapter 18, "Fighting for Freedom." Ask for an oral narration.

Grades 4–6: Read with your older children or assign as independent reading *The Sign of the Beaver*, chapter 14. Ask for an oral or written narration if desired.

Grades 7–9: Read with your older children or assign as independent reading *Carry On, Mr. Bowditch*, chapter 14, "Nineteen Guns." Ask for an oral or written narration if desired.

TERM 2

Book of Centuries Timeline

Paul Revere's Ride, Battles of Lexington and Concord (1775)

Declaration of Independence (1776)

Battle of Bunker Hill (1775)

Washington crosses the Delaware (1776)

Grades 10–12: Read with your older children or assign as independent reading *The Boys of '76,* chapter 14, "Fort Schuyler." Ask for an oral or written narration.

Also read with your older children or assign as independent reading *American Voices,* pages 47 and 48, "The Crisis (excerpts)," and ask for a narration.

Lesson 93: Seventy-two days without a port & Hebrews

Materials Needed
- *Sailing Alone Around the World*
- Outline map of Australia; labeled world map
- Bible
- *Jesus Is Better: Lessons from Hebrews*

Family Geography Book: Ask students what they recall about Joshua Slocum's voyage from the Juan Fernandez islands to the Marquesas islands. See if students can trace on the world map from Boston to Nova Scotia to the Azores to Gibraltar to Pernambuco to Rio de Janeiro to Uruguay to Buenos Aires to the Strait of Magellan to Juan Fernandez islands to the Marquesas islands. Read together *Sailing Alone Around the World,* the first half of chapter 12, and ask for an oral narration.

Family Map Drill: Give each student a copy of an outline map of Australia. Encourage them to label all the states or territories that they know on the map. Compare their labeled states and territories with a labeled world map and make any necessary corrections. Then have them label one or two more states or territories on their maps, copying the spelling and locations from the labeled world map.

Family Bible Study: Complete *Jesus Is Better: Lessons from Hebrews,* lesson 7. Older students and adults may do the Additional Studies section, as well.

Lesson 94: Peter Brings Europe to Russia

Materials Needed
- *Stories of the Nations, Volume 1*
- *Peter the Great* (grades 1–3)
- *The Ocean of Truth* (grades 4–6)
- *The World of William Penn* (grades 7–12)
- *Kidnapped* (grades 7–9)
- *Waverley, Volume 1* (grades 10–12)

Family: Ask students what they recall from last time's reading about Isaac Newton. Write "Peter the Great, czar of Russia" on a whiteboard or sheet of paper. Read together *Stories of the Nations, Volume 1*, chapter 12, "Peter Brings Europe to Russia." Use the map on page 157 to give students an idea of how large Russia was and how far Peter traveled in Europe. Ask for an oral narration.

Grades 1–3: Read together *Peter the Great*, pages 4–11. Ask for an oral narration.

Grades 4–6: Read with your older children or assign as independent reading *The Ocean of Truth*, chapters 2 and 3, "An Ocean Story" and "A Fast." Ask for an oral or written narration.

Grades 7–12: Read with your older children or assign as independent reading *The World of William Penn*, part 6, "Continuing the Life Story of William Penn." Ask for an oral or written narration.

Grades 7–9: Also assign as independent reading *Kidnapped*, chapter 15, "The Lad with the Silver Button: Through the Isle of Mull."

Grades 10–12: Also assign as independent reading *Waverley, Volume 1*, chapter 17, "The Hold of a Highland Robber."

Reminder: Get the book Hearts and Hands: Chronicles of the Awakening Church *for grades 7–12 for lesson 104. Also get a copy of "Sinners in the Hands of an Angry God" by Jonathan Edwards for grades 10–12 to read for lesson 104. If you have a copy of* American Voices, *the sermon is on pages 20–29. If you do not have that book, you can find the sermon online by performing an Internet search. And get* Can't You Make Them Behave, King George? *for grades 1–3 for lesson 105.*

Peter the Great brings Europe to Russia (1682–1725)

Lesson 95: In Isaac Newton's Day, part 1

Materials Needed
- *Peter the Great* (grades 1–3)
- *The Ocean of Truth* (grades 4–6)
- *The World of William Penn* (grades 7–12)
- *Kidnapped* (grades 7–9)
- *Waverley, Volume 1* (grades 10–12)

Grades 1–3: Ask students what they recall from last time's reading about Peter the Great. Read together *Peter the Great*, pages 12–19. Ask for an oral narration.

Grades 4–6: Read with your older children or assign as independent reading *The Ocean of Truth*, chapters 4 and 5, "School" and "A Comet." Ask for an oral or written narration.

Grades 7–12: Read with your older children or assign as independent reading *The World of William Penn,* part 7, "Introducing K'ang-Hse." Ask for an oral or written narration.

Tip: The spelling of "K'ang-Hse" in The World of William Penn *is an alternate to "Kangxi," as given in the* Stories of the Nations, Volume 1, *chapter 9. It is the same ruler.*

Grades 7–9: Also assign as independent reading *Kidnapped,* chapters 16 and 17, "The Lad with the Silver Button: Across Morven" and "The Death of the Red Fox."

Grades 10–12: Also assign as independent reading *Waverley, Volume 1,* chapters 18 and 19, "Waverley Proceeds on His Journey" and "The Chief and His Mansion."

Tip: Make sure older children are up to date with their Book of Centuries entries.

 # Lesson 96: Early America, part 7

Materials Needed
- *Toliver's Secret* (grades 1–3)
- *The Sign of the Beaver* (grades 4–6)
- *Carry On, Mr. Bowditch* (grades 7–9)
- *The Boys of '76* (grades 10–12)
- *American Voices* (grades 10–12)

Grades 1–3: Read together *Toliver's Secret,* chapter 1.

Grades 4–6: Read with your older children or assign as independent reading *The Sign of the Beaver,* chapter 15. Ask for an oral or written narration if desired.

Grades 7–9: Read with your older children or assign as independent reading *Carry On, Mr. Bowditch,* chapter 15, "Sail Ho-o-o-o-o." Ask for an oral or written narration if desired.

Grades 10–12: Read with your older children or assign as independent reading *The Boys of '76,* chapter 15, "Bennington." Ask for an oral or written narration.

Also read with your older children or assign as independent reading *American Voices,* pages 49–54, "Articles of Confederation," and ask for a narration.

 # Lesson 97: Early America, part 8

Materials Needed
- *Toliver's Secret* (grades 1–3)

- *The Sign of the Beaver* (grades 4–6)
- *Carry On, Mr. Bowditch* (grades 7–9)
- *The Boys of '76* (grades 10–12)

Grades 1–3: Read together *Toliver's Secret*, chapter 2.

Grades 4–6: Read with your older children or assign as independent reading *The Sign of the Beaver,* chapter 16. Ask for an oral or written narration if desired.

Grades 7–9: Read with your older children or assign as independent reading *Carry On, Mr. Bowditch,* chapter 16, "A Simple Matter of Mathematics." Ask for an oral or written narration if desired.

Grades 10–12: Read with your older children or assign as independent reading *The Boys of '76,* chapter 16, "Brandywine." Ask for an oral or written narration.

Lesson 98: Samoan hospitality & Hebrews

Materials Needed
- *Sailing Alone Around the World*
- Outline map of Australia; labeled world map
- Bible
- *Jesus Is Better: Lessons from Hebrews*

Family Geography Book: See if students can trace on the world map from Boston to Nova Scotia to the Azores to Gibraltar to Pernambuco to Rio de Janeiro to Uruguay to Buenos Aires to the Strait of Magellan to Juan Fernandez islands to the Marquesas islands. Ask students what they recall about Joshua Slocum's sailing for 72 days without a port. Read together *Sailing Alone Around the World,* the last half of chapter 12, and ask for an oral narration.

Family Map Drill: Give each student a copy of an outline map of Australia. Encourage them to label all the states or territories that they know on the map. Compare their labeled states and territories with a labeled world map and make any necessary corrections. Then have them label one or two more states or territories on their maps, copying the spelling and locations from the labeled world map.

Family Bible Study: Complete *Jesus Is Better: Lessons from Hebrews,* lesson 8. Older students and adults may do the Additional Studies section, as well.

Lesson 99: In Isaac Newton's Day, part 2

Materials Needed
- *Peter the Great* (grades 1–3)

• *The Ocean of Truth* (grades 4–6)
• *The World of William Penn* (grades 7–12)
• *Kidnapped* (grades 7–9)
• *Waverley, Volume 1* (grades 10–12)

Grades 1–3: Ask students what they recall from last time's reading about Peter the Great. Read together *Peter the Great*, pages 20–25. Ask for an oral narration.

Grades 4–6: Read with your older children or assign as independent reading *The Ocean of Truth*, chapters 6 and 7, "Pax" and "Saying Good-bye." Ask for an oral or written narration.

Grades 7–12: Read with your older children or assign as independent reading *The World of William Penn*, part 8, "Introducing Peter the Great." Ask for an oral or written narration.

Grades 7–9: Also assign as independent reading *Kidnapped*, chapter 18, "I Talk with Alan in the Wood of Lettermore."

Grades 10–12: Also assign as independent reading *Waverley, Volume 1*, chapters 20 and 21, "A Highland Feast" and "The Chieftain's Sister."

 # Lesson 100: In Isaac Newton's Day, part 3

Materials Needed
• *Peter the Great* (grades 1–3)
• *The Ocean of Truth* (grades 4–6)
• *The World of William Penn* (grades 7–12)
• *Kidnapped* (grades 7–9)
• *Waverley, Volume 1* (grades 10–12)

Grades 1–3: Ask students what they recall from last time's reading about Peter the Great. Read together *Peter the Great*, pages 26–32. Ask for an oral narration.

Grades 4–6: Read with your older children or assign as independent reading *The Ocean of Truth*, chapters 8 and 9, "A Young Farmer" and "The Great Ocean." Ask for an oral or written narration.

Grades 7–12: Read with your older children or assign as independent reading *The World of William Penn*, part 9, "Concluding the Life Story of William Penn." Ask for an oral or written narration.

Grades 7–9: Also assign as independent reading *Kidnapped*, chapters 19 and 20, "The House of Fear" and "The Flight in the Heather: the Rocks."

Grades 10–12: Also assign as independent reading *Waverley, Volume 1*, chapters 22 and 23, "Highland Minstrelsy" and "Waverley Continues at Glennaquoich."

Tip: Make sure older children are up to date with their Book of Centuries entries.

Lesson 101: Early America, part 9

Materials Needed
- *Toliver's Secret* (grades 1–3)
- *The Sign of the Beaver* (grades 4–6)
- *Carry On, Mr. Bowditch* (grades 7–9)
- *The Boys of '76* (grades 10–12)

Grades 1–3: Read together *Toliver's Secret*, chapter 3.

Grades 4–6: Read with your older children or assign as independent reading *The Sign of the Beaver*, chapter 17. Ask for an oral or written narration if desired.

Grades 7–9: Read with your older children or assign as independent reading *Carry On, Mr. Bowditch*, chapter 17, "Lunars and Moonlight." Ask for an oral or written narration if desired.

Grades 10–12: Read with your older children or assign as independent reading *The Boys of '76*, chapter 17, "Stillwater." Ask for an oral or written narration.

 # Lesson 102: Early America, part 10

Materials Needed
- *Toliver's Secret* (grades 1–3)
- *The Sign of the Beaver* (grades 4–6)
- *Carry On, Mr. Bowditch* (grades 7–9)
- *The Boys of '76* (grades 10–12)

Grades 1–3: Read together *Toliver's Secret*, chapter 4.

Grades 4–6: Read with your older children or assign as independent reading *The Sign of the Beaver*, chapter 18. Ask for an oral or written narration if desired.

Grades 7–9: Read with your older children or assign as independent reading *Carry On, Mr. Bowditch*, chapter 18, "The Astrea to the Rescue." Ask for an oral or written narration if desired.

Grades 10–12: Read with your older children or assign as independent reading *The Boys of '76*, chapter 18, "Germantown." Ask for an oral or written narration.

 # Lesson 103: Samoan royalty & Hebrews

Materials Needed
- *Sailing Alone Around the World*
- Outline map of Australia; labeled world map

• Bible
• *Jesus Is Better: Lessons from Hebrews*

Family Geography Book: See if students can trace on the world map from Boston to Nova Scotia to the Azores to Gibraltar to Pernambuco to Rio de Janeiro to Uruguay to Buenos Aires to the Strait of Magellan to Juan Fernandez islands to the Marquesas islands to Samoa. Ask students what they recall about Joshua Slocum's time in Samoa so far. Read together *Sailing Alone Around the World*, the first half of chapter 13, and ask for an oral narration.

Family Map Drill: Give each student a copy of an outline map of Australia. Encourage them to label all the states or territories that they know on the map. Compare their labeled states and territories with a labeled world map and make any necessary corrections. Then have them label one or two more states or territories on their maps, copying the spelling and locations from the labeled world map.

Family Bible Study: Complete *Jesus Is Better: Lessons from Hebrews*, lesson 9. Older students and adults may do the Additional Studies section, as well.

Lesson 104: The Great Lisbon Earthquake

Materials Needed
• *Stories of the Nations, Volume 1*
• *The Ocean of Truth* (grades 4–6)
• *Hearts and Hands* (grades 7–12)
• *Kidnapped* (grades 7–9)
• "Sinners in the Hands of an Angry God" (grades 10–12)

Great Lisbon earthquake (1755)

Family: Read together *Stories of the Nations, Volume 1*, chapter 13, "The Great Lisbon Earthquake." Use the map on page 157 to locate Lisbon, Portugal. Ask for an oral narration.

Grades 4–6: Read with your older children or assign as independent reading *The Ocean of Truth*, chapter 10, "The University on the River Cam." Ask for an oral or written narration.

Grades 7–12: Read with your older children or assign as independent reading *Hearts and Hands*, "What was the Awakening Church?" and "Jonathan Edwards." Ask for an oral or written narration.

Grades 7–9: Also assign as independent reading *Kidnapped*, chapter 21, "The Flight in the Heather: the Heugh of Corrynakiegh."

Grades 10–12: Also assign as independent reading the Jonathan Edwards sermon, "Sinners in the Hands of an Angry God." If you already have a copy of *American Voices,* you will find the sermon on pages 20–29, or you can easily find it online by doing an Internet search.

 ## Lesson 105: Captain Cook Explores the Unknown

Materials Needed
- *Stories of the Nations, Volume 1*
- *Can't You Make Them Behave, King George?* (grades 1–3)
- *The Ocean of Truth* (grades 4–6)
- *Hearts and Hands* (grades 7–12)
- *Kidnapped* (grades 7–9)
- *Waverley, Volume 1* (grades 10–12)

Family: Ask students what they recall from last time's reading about the Lisbon earthquake. Write "incognita" on a small whiteboard or sheet of paper. Ask students if any of them know or want to guess what that word means. Read together *Stories of the Nations, Volume 1*, chapter 14, "Captain Cook Explores the Unknown." Use the map on page 165 to trace Cook's explorations. Ask for an oral narration.

Grades 1–3: Show students the title of the book *Can't You Make Them Behave, King George?* and explain that it is about the man who was king of England while Captain Cook was exploring the unknown. Read together *Can't You Make Them Behave, King George?*, pages 6–15. Ask for an oral narration.

Grades 4–6: Read with your older children or assign as independent reading *The Ocean of Truth*, chapter 11, "Questions." Ask for an oral or written narration.

Grades 7–12: Read with your older children or assign as independent reading *Hearts and Hands*, "Johann Sebastian Bach" and "The Development of Church Music." Ask for an oral or written narration.

Grades 7–9: Also assign as independent reading *Kidnapped*, chapter 22, "The Flight in the Heather: the Moor."

Grades 10–12: Also assign as independent reading *Waverley, Volume 1*, chapter 24, "Stag-Hunt and Its Consequences."

Tip: Make sure older children are up to date with their Book of Centuries entries.

Captain James Cook explores the unknown (1728–1779)

Lesson 106: Early America, part 11

Materials Needed
- *Toliver's Secret* (grades 1–3)

• *The Sign of the Beaver* (grades 4–6)
• *Carry On, Mr. Bowditch* (grades 7–9)
• *The Boys of '76* (grades 10–12)

Grades 1–3: Read together *Toliver's Secret,* chapter 5.

Grades 4–6: Read with your older children or assign as independent reading *The Sign of the Beaver,* chapter 19. Ask for an oral or written narration if desired.

Grades 7–9: Read with your older children or assign as independent reading *Carry On, Mr. Bowditch,* chapter 19, "Strange Sailing Orders." Ask for an oral or written narration if desired.

Grades 10–12: Read with your older children or assign as independent reading *The Boys of '76,* chapter 19, "The Highlands of the Hudson." Ask for an oral or written narration.

Lesson 107: Early America, part 12

Materials Needed
• *Toliver's Secret* (grades 1–3)
• *The Sign of the Beaver* (grades 4–6)
• *Carry On, Mr. Bowditch* (grades 7–9)
• *The Boys of '76* (grades 10–12)

Grades 1–3: Read together *Toliver's Secret,* chapter 6.

Grades 4–6: Read with your older children or assign as independent reading *The Sign of the Beaver,* chapter 20. Ask for an oral or written narration if desired.

Grades 7–9: Read with your older children or assign as independent reading *Carry On, Mr. Bowditch,* chapter 20, "Book Sailing." Ask for an oral or written narration if desired.

Grades 10–12: Read with your older children or assign as independent reading *The Boys of '76,* chapter 20, "Saratoga." Ask for an oral or written narration.

Lesson 108: In Tasmania & Hebrews

Materials Needed
• *Sailing Alone Around the World*
• Outline map of Australia; labeled world map
• Bible
• *Jesus Is Better: Lessons from Hebrews*

Family Geography Book: Ask students what they recall about Joshua Slocum's voyage to Fiji and Australia. Read together *Sailing Alone Around the World*, the last half of chapter 13, and ask for an oral narration. See if students can trace on the world map from Boston to Nova Scotia to the Azores to Gibraltar to Pernambuco to Rio de Janeiro to Uruguay to Buenos Aires to the Strait of Magellan to Juan Fernandez islands to the Marquesas islands to Samoa to Fiji to Australia to Tasmania.

Family Map Drill: Give each student a copy of an outline map of Australia. Encourage them to label all the states or territories that they know on the map. Compare their labeled states and territories with a labeled world map and make any necessary corrections. Then have them label one or two more states or territories on their maps, copying the spelling and locations from the labeled world map.

Family Bible Study: Complete *Jesus Is Better: Lessons from Hebrews*, lesson 10. Older students and adults may do the Additional Studies section, as well.

 ## Lesson 109: In Isaac Newton's Day, part 4

Materials Needed
- *Can't You Make Them Behave, King George?* (grades 1–3)
- *The Ocean of Truth* (grades 4–6)
- *Hearts and Hands* (grades 7–12)
- *Kidnapped* (grades 7–9)
- *Waverley, Volume 1* (grades 10–12)

Grades 1–3: Ask students what they recall from last time's reading about King George. Read together *Can't You Make Them Behave, King George?*, pages 16–27. Ask for an oral narration.

Grades 4–6: Read with your older children or assign as independent reading *The Ocean of Truth*, chapters 12 and 13, "The Apple and the Moon" and "Chemistry." Ask for an oral or written narration.

Grades 7–12: Read with your older children or assign as independent reading *Hearts and Hands*, "John Wesley." Ask for an oral or written narration.

Grades 7–9: Also assign as independent reading *Kidnapped*, chapters 23 and 24, "Cluny's Cage" and "The Flight in the Heather: the Quarrel."

Grades 10–12: Also assign as independent reading *Waverley, Volume 1*, chapters 25 and 26, "News from England" and "An Eclaircissement."

 ## Lesson 110: In Isaac Newton's Day, part 5

Materials Needed
- *Can't You Make Them Behave, King George?* (grades 1–3)

- *The Ocean of Truth* (grades 4–6)
- *Hearts and Hands* (grades 7–12)
- *Kidnapped* (grades 7–9)
- *Waverley, Volume 1* (grades 10–12)

Grades 1–3: Ask students what they recall from last time's reading about King George. Read together *Can't You Make Them Behave, King George?*, pages 28–35. Ask for an oral narration.

Grades 4–6: Read with your older children or assign as independent reading *The Ocean of Truth,* chapters 14 and 15, "Subject to the Dominion of One" and "Beginning with Noah." Ask for an oral or written narration.

Grades 7–12: Read with your older children or assign as independent reading *Hearts and Hands,* "An Era of Social Reform" and "William Wilberforce and the Abolitionists." Ask for an oral or written narration.

Grades 7–9: Also assign as independent reading *Kidnapped*, chapters 25 and 26, "In Balquhidder" and "End of the Flight: We Pass the Forth."

Grades 10–12: Also assign as independent reading *Waverley, Volume 1,* chapters 27 and 28, "Upon the Same Subject" and "A Letter from Tully-Veolan."

Reminder: Start gathering the resources you will need for Term 3. See page 103.

 Lesson 111: Early America, part 13

Materials Needed
- *Toliver's Secret* (grades 1–3)
- *The Sign of the Beaver* (grades 4–6)
- *Carry On, Mr. Bowditch* (grades 7–9)
- *The Boys of '76* (grades 10–12)

Grades 1–3: Read together *Toliver's Secret*, chapter 7.

Grades 4–6: Read with your older children or assign as independent reading *The Sign of the Beaver,* chapter 21. Ask for an oral or written narration if desired.

Grades 7–9: Read with your older children or assign as independent reading *Carry On, Mr. Bowditch,* chapter 21, "Sealing Is Safer." Ask for an oral or written narration if desired.

Grades 10–12: Read with your older children or assign as independent reading *The Boys of '76,* chapter 21, "Operations on the Delaware." Ask for an oral or written narration.

Reminder: If you want to do the optional hands-on project for lesson 117, start collecting the materials you will need.

 Lesson 112: Early America, part 14

Materials Needed
- *Toliver's Secret* (grades 1–3)
- *The Sign of the Beaver* (grades 4–6)
- *Carry On, Mr. Bowditch* (grades 7–9)
- *The Boys of '76* (grades 10–12)

Grades 1–3: Read together *Toliver's Secret*, chapter 8. (Note: Students will finish *Toliver's Secret* next term.)

Grades 4–6: Read with your older children or assign as independent reading *The Sign of the Beaver*, chapters 22 and 23. Ask for an oral or written narration if desired.

Grades 7–9: Read with your older children or assign as independent reading *Carry On, Mr. Bowditch*, chapter 22, "Science and Sumatra." Ask for an oral or written narration if desired.

Grades 10–12: Read with your older children or assign as independent reading *The Boys of '76,* chapter 22, "Valley Forge and Philadelphia." Ask for an oral or written narration. (Note: Students will finish *The Boys of '76* next term.)

 Lesson 113: Cruising round Tasmania & Hebrews

Materials Needed
- *Sailing Alone Around the World*
- Outline map of Australia; labeled world map
- Bible
- *Jesus Is Better: Lessons from Hebrews*

Family Geography Book: See if students can trace on the world map from Boston to Nova Scotia to the Azores to Gibraltar to Pernambuco to Rio de Janeiro to Uruguay to Buenos Aires to the Strait of Magellan to Juan Fernandez islands to the Marquesas islands to Samoa to Fiji to Australia. Ask students what they recall about Joshua Slocum's time near Australia so far. Read together *Sailing Alone Around the World*, the first half of chapter 14, and ask for an oral narration.

Family Map Drill: Give each student a copy of an outline map of Australia.

Book of Centuries Timeline

Encourage them to label all the states or territories that they know on the map. Compare their labeled states and territories with a labeled world map and make any necessary corrections. Then have them label one or two more states or territories on their maps, copying the spelling and locations from the labeled world map.

Family Bible Study: Complete *Jesus Is Better: Lessons from Hebrews*, lesson 11. Older students and adults may do the Additional Studies section, as well.

Lesson 114: In Isaac Newton's Day, part 6

Materials Needed
- *Can't You Make Them Behave, King George?* (grades 1–3)
- *The Ocean of Truth* (grades 4–6)
- *Hearts and Hands* (grades 7–12)
- *Kidnapped* (grades 7–9)
- *Waverley, Volume 1* (grades 10–12)

Grades 1–3: Ask students what they recall from last time's reading about King George. Read together *Can't You Make Them Behave, King George?*, pages 36–46. Ask for an oral narration.

Tip: The final sentence of the book is most likely not historically accurate, though it probably sums up King George's frustration with the American colonists. Omit it if desired.

Grades 4–6: Read with your older children or assign as independent reading *The Ocean of Truth*, chapters 16 and 17, "Detective at the Mint" and "Sir Isaac." Ask for an oral or written narration.

Grades 7–12: Read with your older children or assign as independent reading *Hearts and Hands*, "William Carey." Ask for an oral or written narration.

Grades 7–9: Also assign as independent reading *Kidnapped*, chapters 27 and 28, "I Come to Mr. Rankeillor" and "I Go in Quest of My Inheritance."

Grades 10–12: Also assign as independent reading *Waverley, Volume 1*, chapter 29, "Waverley's Reception in the Lowlands."

Lesson 115: Catherine Makes More Changes

Materials Needed
- *Stories of the Nations, Volume 1*
- *The Ocean of Truth* (grades 4–6)

- *Hearts and Hands* (grades 7–12)
- *Kidnapped* (grades 7–9)
- *Waverley, Volume 1* (grades 10–12)

Family: Read together *Stories of the Nations, Volume 1*, chapter 15, "Catherine Makes More Changes." If you compare the maps on pages 157 and 161, you can see which parts of Poland were divided among the three countries mentioned. The map on page 157 will show Crimea. Ask for an oral narration.

Grades 4–6: Read with your older children or assign as independent reading *The Ocean of Truth*, chapter 18, "Final Causes," and the Epilogue. Ask for an oral or written narration.

Grades 7–12: Read with your older children or assign as independent reading *Hearts and Hands*, "Elizabeth Fry." Ask for an oral or written narration. (Note: Students will finish this book next term.)

Grades 7–9: Also assign as independent reading *Kidnapped*, chapters 29 and 30, "I Come into My Kingdom" and "Good-Bye."

Grades 10–12: Also assign as independent reading *Waverley, Volume 1*, "Author's Note." Or use today to catch up on any reading assignments in *Waverley*.

Tip: *Students in grades 10–12 may wish to read* Waverley, Volume 2, *in their leisure time.*

Tip: *Make sure older children are up to date with their Book of Centuries entries. They may want to add entries for the people about whom they read in* Hearts and Hands *this term. You will find a timeline on pages 8 and 9 of that book.*

Book of Centuries Timeline

Catherine the Great rules Russia (1762–1796)

Lesson 116: American History Exam

Materials Needed

- *The Sign of the Beaver* (grades 4–6)
- *Carry On, Mr. Bowditch* (grades 7–9)

Family: Use the questions below to begin the students' exam on Early American history.

Tip: *Exams in a Charlotte Mason school require no "cramming" or preparation. You may be pleasantly surprised at what your students remember with no prompting.*

Grades 1–3: Tell the story of Sarah Noble.
Grades 4–6: Tell the history of the "shot heard 'round the world."

Grades 7–9: Describe George Washington, his work and his character, as shown from his teen years, his efforts in the French and Indian War, and his command of Revolutionary troops.

Grades 10–12: Explain how the colonists' relationship with England changed over the course of the years. What factors affected that change?

Tip: You may want to assign the older students to write their exam answers. Younger students may do oral exams; you might want to write or type their answers as they tell what they know. Or, if you have students in more than one grade level, you might allow them to do their exams orally in a group. That way the older can hear the younger, and the younger can hear the older.

Grades 4–6: Read with your older children or assign as independent reading *The Sign of the Beaver,* chapter 24. Ask for an oral or written narration if desired.

Grades 7–9: Read with your older children or assign as independent reading *Carry On, Mr. Bowditch,* chapter 23, "Captain Bowditch Commanding." Ask for an oral or written narration if desired.

Lesson 117: American History Project or Exam

Materials Needed
   • (optional) Materials for hands-on project
   • *The Sign of the Beaver* (grades 4–6)
   • *Carry On, Mr. Bowditch* (grades 7–9)

Family: Do a hands-on project (see below), or use the questions below to continue the students' exam on Early American history.

Grades 1–3: What is a colonist? What colonists have you heard of? Tell about one.

Grades 4–6: Tell what the colonists thought about Indians and what Indians thought about the colonists.

Grades 7–9: Describe how Nat Bowditch's calculations and discoveries changed the navigation of ships.

Grades 10–12: Compare and contrast the military techniques of the British and the colonists, citing examples from the battles you have read about.

Optional Hands-On Project: Select a hands-on project from the Links and Tips page: http://SimplyCharlotteMason.com/books/early-modern/links-tips/

Grades 4–6: Read with your older children or assign as independent reading *The Sign of the Beaver,* chapter 25. Ask for an oral or written narration if desired.

Grades 7–9: Read with your older children or assign as independent reading *Carry On, Mr. Bowditch,* chapter 24, "Man Against the Fog." Ask for an oral or written narration if desired.

Lesson 118: Friends on the Australian coast & Bible Exam

Materials Needed
- *Sailing Alone Around the World*
- Labeled world map

Family Geography Book: Ask students what they recall about Joshua Slocum's lecturing in Tasmania. Read together *Sailing Alone Around the World,* the last half of chapter 14, and ask for an oral narration. See if students can trace on the world map from Boston to Nova Scotia to the Azores to Gibraltar to Pernambuco to Rio de Janeiro to Uruguay to Buenos Aires to the Strait of Magellan to Juan Fernandez islands to the Marquesas islands to Samoa to Fiji to Australia (Melbourne, Tasmania, and Sydney).

Bible Exam: Use the questions below for the students' exam on Hebrews.

Grades 1–3: Tell what the book of Hebrews is about.
Grades 4–6: Give the background of the book of Hebrews and explain why the writer wanted to show that Jesus is better.
Grades 7–9: Select two of these comparisons given in Hebrews and describe how Jesus is better: angels, Moses, the high priest, the Old Covenant sacrifices.
Grades 10–12: Describe how Jesus is better than angels, Moses, the high priest, and the Old Covenant sacrifices.

Tip: If you assigned Scripture memory from Hebrews, you might also ask for a recitation of the passage(s). Be sure to encourage the children to say beautiful words in a beautiful way as they recite.

 # Lesson 119: World History Exam

Family: Use the questions below for the students' exam on Early Modern world history.

Grades 1–3: Tell a story from this term about a king.
Grades 4–6: Tell about an explorer of whom you read this term.
Grades 7–9: Tell the story of William Penn and two other people who lived during his lifetime: Marquette, Louis XIV, Isaac Newton, K'ang-Hse (also known as Kangxi), Peter the Great.
Grades 10–12: Of all the rulers about whom you have read so far in your

study of Early Modern world history, which one do you consider the greatest? Explain your reasoning, citing examples from your reading, and include any ways that you would disagree with him/her.

Lesson 120: World History Exam

Family: Use the questions below for the students' exam on Early Modern world history.

Grades 1–3: Tell a story from this term about someone who helped others.
Grades 4–6: Tell all you know about Isaac Newton.
Grades 7–12: What is meant by the "Awakening Church" during this time period? Give three examples from your church history reading to support your definition.

Term 3

(12 weeks; 5 lessons/week)

American History Resources

- *Stories of America, Volume 1,* by Charles Morris and Sonya Shafer

Grades 1–3
- *Toliver's Secret* by Esther Wood Brady
- *Benjamin Franklin* by Ingri and Edgar Parin D'Aulaire

Grades 4–6
- *A Young Patriot: The American Revolution as Experienced by One Boy* by Jim Murphy
- *Amos Fortune, Free Man* by Elizabeth Yates

Grades 7–9
- *Early Thunder* by Jean Fritz OR *Johnny Tremain* by Esther Forbes
- *Lewis and Clark: The Journey of the Corps of Discovery* by Dayton Duncan and Ken Burns
- Book of Centuries (one for each student)

Grades 10–12
- *The Boys of '76* by Charles Coffin
- *American Voices* edited by Ray Notgrass
- *Lewis and Clark: The Journey of the Corps of Discovery* by Dayton Duncan and Ken Burns
- Book of Centuries (one for each student)

Optional Resources
- Dover Coloring Books
    Heroes and Heroines of the American Revolution
    Story of the American Revolution
- Various resources for optional hands-on projects

World History, Bible, Geography Resources

- *Stories of the Nations, Volume 1,* by Charles Morris, Lorene Lambert, and Sonya Shafer
- *GOAL Bible Study Journal* by Sonya Shafer
- Bible
- *Sailing Alone Around the World* by Joshua Slocum
- *Uncle Josh's Outline Map book or CD* by George and Hannah Wiggers (or other outline maps of Australia and Central America)
- Labeled world map

Grades 1–3
- *Out of Darkness: The Story of Louis Braille* by Russell Freedman

Grades 4–6
- *The Story of Napoleon* by H. E. Marshall

Grades 7–9
- *The Year of the Horseless Carriage* by Genevieve Foster
- *The Story of Modern France* by H. A. Guerber
- *Hearts and Hands: Chronicles of the Awakening Church* by Mindy and Brandon Withrow

- *Lafayette and the American Revolution* by Russell Freedman
- *Discovering Doctrine* by Sonya Shafer (one for each student)
- Book of Centuries (one for each student)

Grades 10–12

- *The Year of the Horseless Carriage* by Genevieve Foster
- *A Tale of Two Cities* by Charles Dickens
- *Hearts and Hands: Chronicles of the Awakening Church* by Mindy and Brandon Withrow
- *Lafayette and the American Revolution* by Russell Freedman
- *Discovering Doctrine* by Sonya Shafer (one for each student)
- Book of Centuries (one for each student)

	Family	Grades 1–3	Grades 4–6	Grades 7–9	Grades 10–12
Week 1					
Bible	1 Timothy 1				
World History	Stories of the Nations, Vol. 1, ch. 16, 17			The Year of the Horseless Carriage, pp. 11–42; The Story of Modern France, ch. 1, 2	The Year of the Horseless Carriage, pp. 11–42; A Tale of Two Cities, Book 1, ch. 1–4
Geography	Sailing Alone Around the World, ch. 15A; Map Drill: Australia				
American History		Toliver's Secret, ch. 9, 10	A Young Patriot, ch. 1, 2	Early Thunder, ch. 1–3 OR Johnny Tremain, ch. 1, 2	The Boys of '76, ch. 23, 24
Week 2					
Bible	1 Timothy 2, 3				
World History	Stories of the Nations, Vol. 1, ch. 18, 19			The Year of the Horseless Carriage, pp. 43–71; The Story of Modern France, ch. 3, 4	The Year of the Horseless Carriage, pp. 43–71; A Tale of Two Cities, Book 1, ch. 5, 6; Book 2, ch. 1, 2
Geography	Sailing Alone Around the World, ch. 15B; Map Drill: Australia				
American History		Toliver's Secret, ch. 11, 12	A Young Patriot, ch. 3	Early Thunder, ch. 4–6 OR Johnny Tremain, ch. 3, 4	The Boys of '76, ch. 25, 26
Week 3					
Bible	1 Timothy 4				
World History	Stories of the Nations, Vol. 1, ch. 20, 21		The Story of Napoleon, ch. 1	The Year of the Horseless Carriage, pp. 72–92; The Story of Modern France, ch. 5, 6; Lafayette and the American Revolution, ch. 1	The Year of the Horseless Carriage, pp. 72–92; A Tale of Two Cities, Book 2, ch. 3–6; Lafayette and the American Revolution, ch. 1
Geography	Sailing Alone Around the World, ch. 16A; Map Drill: Australia				
American History	Stories of America, Vol. 1, ch. 19	Toliver's Secret, ch. 13	A Young Patriot, ch. 4	Early Thunder, ch. 7–9 OR Johnny Tremain, ch. 5, 6	The Boys of '76, ch. 27, 28
Week 4					
Bible	1 Timothy 5				
World History		Out of Darkness, ch. 1, 2	The Story of Napoleon, ch. 2, 3	Lafayette and the Am. Revolution, ch. 2, 3; The Story of Modern France, ch. 7, 8	Lafayette and the American Revolution, ch. 2, 3; A Tale of Two Cities, Book 2, ch. 7–10
Geography	Sailing Alone Around the World, ch. 16B; Map Drill: Central America				
American History	Stories of America, Vol. 1, ch. 20, 21		A Young Patriot, ch. 5A, 5B	Early Thunder, ch. 10, 11 OR Johnny Tremain, ch. 7, 8	The Boys of '76, ch. 29, 30

	Family	Grades 1–3	Grades 4–6	Grades 7–9	Grades 10–12
Week 5					
Bible	1 Timothy 6				
World History		Out of Darkness, ch. 3, 4	The Story of Napoleon, ch. 4, 5	Lafayette and the Am. Revolution, ch. 4, 5; The Story of Modern France, ch. 9, 10	Lafayette and the American Revolution, ch. 4, 5; A Tale of Two Cities, Book 2, ch. 11–14
Geography	Sailing Alone Around the World, ch. 17A; Map Drill: Central America				
American History	Stories of America, Vol. 1, ch. 22, 23		A Young Patriot, ch. 5C, 6A	Early Thunder, ch. 12, 13 OR Johnny Tremain, ch. 9, 10	The Boys of '76, ch. 31, 32; American Voices, pp. 57–71
Week 6					
Bible	Titus 1, 2				
World History		Out of Darkness, ch. 5, 6	The Story of Napoleon, ch. 6, 7	Lafayette and the Am. Revolution, ch. 6, 7; The Story of Modern France, ch. 11, 12	Lafayette and the American Revolution, ch. 6, 7; A Tale of Two Cities, Book 2, ch. 15–18
Geography	Sailing Alone Around the World, ch. 17B; Map Drill: Central America				
American History	Stories of America, Vol. 1, ch. 24	Benjamin Franklin, pp. 2–10	A Young Patriot, ch. 6B–8	Early Thunder, ch. 14 OR Johnny Tremain, ch. 11, 12; Lewis and Clark, ch. 1	The Boys of '76, ch. 33, Conclusion; American Voices, pp. 77–90; Lewis and Clark, ch. 1
Week 7					
Bible	Titus 3				
World History		Out of Darkness, ch. 7, 8	The Story of Napoleon, ch. 8, 9	Lafayette and the Am. Revolution, ch. 8, 9; The Story of Modern France, ch.13, 14	Lafayette and the American Revolution, ch. 8, 9; A Tale of Two Cities, Book 2, ch. 19–22
Geography	Sailing Alone Around the World, ch. 18A; Map Drill: Central America				
American History		Benjamin Franklin, pp. 12–28	Amos Fortune, Free Man, ch. 1–4	Lewis and Clark, ch. 2, 3	Lewis and Clark, ch. 2, 3
Week 8					
Bible	2 Timothy 1				
World History	Stories of the Nations, Vol. 1, ch. 22, 23		The Story of Napoleon, ch. 10	Lafayette and the Am. Revolution, ch. 10; The Story of Modern France, ch. 15, 16; Hearts and Hands	Lafayette and the Am. Revolution, ch. 10; A Tale of Two Cities, Book 2, ch. 23, 24; Book 3, ch. 1, 2; Hearts and Hands
Geography	Sailing Alone Around the World, ch. 18B; Map Drill: Central America				
American History		Benjamin Franklin, pp. 30–48	Amos Fortune, Free Man, ch. 5–8	Lewis and Clark, ch. 4, 5	Lewis and Clark, ch. 4, 5; American Voices, pp. 94–97

	Family	Grades 1–3	Grades 4–6	Grades 7–9	Grades 10–12
Week 9					
Bible	2 Timothy 2				
World History	Stories of the Nations, Vol. 1, ch. 24, 25			Hearts and Hands; The Story of Modern France, ch. 17, 18	Hearts and Hands; A Tale of Two Cities, Book 3, ch. 3–6
Geography	Sailing Alone Around the World, ch. 19; Map Drill: Central America				
American History	Stories of America, Vol. 1, ch. 25, 26		Amos Fortune, Free Man, ch. 9–12	Lewis and Clark, ch. 6, 7	Lewis and Clark, ch. 6, 7; American Voices, pp. 103–106
Week 10					
Bible	2 Timothy 3				
World History	Stories of the Nations, Vol. 1, ch. 26, 27			Hearts and Hands; The Story of Modern France, ch. 19, 20	Hearts and Hands; A Tale of Two Cities, Book 3, ch. 7–10
Geography	Sailing Alone Around the World, ch. 20; Map Drill: Central America				
American History	Stories of America, Vol. 1, New England Boy's poem, ch. 27		Amos Fortune, Free Man, ch. 13–16	Lewis and Clark, ch. 8, 9	Lewis and Clark, ch. 8, 9; American Voices, pp. 108–110
Week 11					
Bible	2 Timothy 4				
World History	Stories of the Nations, Vol. 1, ch. 28; Catch up			Hearts and Hands; The Story of Modern France, ch. 21–23	Hearts and Hands; A Tale of Two Cities, Book 3, ch. 11–15
Geography	Sailing Alone Around the World, ch. 21; Map Drill: Central America				
American History	Stories of America, Vol. 1, ch. 28, 29		Amos Fortune, Free Man, ch. 17–20	Lewis and Clark, ch. 10, 11	Lewis and Clark, ch. 10, 11; American Voices, pp. 128–130, 134–136
Week 12					
Bible	Exam				
World History	Exam				
Geography	Exam				
American History	Exam or Project		Catch Up	Lewis and Clark, ch. 12	Lewis and Clark, ch. 12

Lesson 121: Revolutionary Times, part 1

Materials Needed
- *Toliver's Secret* (grades 1–3)
- *A Young Patriot* (grades 4–6)
- *Early Thunder* OR *Johnny Tremain* (grades 7–9)
- *The Boys of '76* (grades 10–12)

Grades 1–3: Ask students to recall what has happened so far in *Toliver's Secret*. Read together *Toliver's Secret*, chapter 9.

Grades 4–6: Read with your older children or assign as independent reading *A Young Patriot,* chapter 1, "The Smell of War." Ask for an oral or written narration.

Grades 7–9: Read with your older children or assign as independent reading *Early Thunder,* chapters 1 and 2, OR *Johnny Tremain*, chapter 1. (See page 15 for details that might help in deciding which book to use.) Ask for an oral or written narration if desired.

Grades 10–12: Read with your older children or assign as independent reading *The Boys of '76*, chapter 23, "Stony Point." Ask for an oral or written narration.

 Lesson 122: Revolutionary Times, part 2

Materials Needed
- *Toliver's Secret* (grades 1–3)
- *A Young Patriot* (grades 4–6)
- *Early Thunder* OR *Johnny Tremain* (grades 7–9)
- *The Boys of '76* (grades 10–12)

Grades 1–3: Read together *Toliver's Secret*, chapter 10.

Grades 4–6: Read with your older children or assign as independent reading *A Young Patriot,* chapter 2, "Now I Was a Soldier." Ask for an oral or written narration.

Grades 7–9: Read with your older children or assign as independent reading *Early Thunder,* chapter 3, OR *Johnny Tremain*, chapter 2. Ask for an oral or written narration if desired.

Grades 10–12: Read with your older children or assign as independent reading *The Boys of '76*, chapter 24, "Monmouth." Ask for an oral or written narration.

 Lesson 123: Arrival at Port Denison & 1 Timothy 1

Materials Needed
- *Sailing Alone Around the World*

Book of Centuries Timeline

• Outline map of Australia; labeled world map
• Bible
• *GOAL Bible Study Journal*
• *Discovering Doctrine* (grades 7–12)

Family Geography Book: Ask students what they recall about Joshua Slocum's stay in Australia so far. Read together *Sailing Alone Around the World*, the first half of chapter 15, and ask for an oral narration. See if students can trace on the world map from Boston to Nova Scotia to the Azores to Gibraltar to Pernambuco to Rio de Janeiro to Uruguay to Buenos Aires to the Strait of Magellan to Juan Fernandez islands to the Marquesas islands to Samoa to Fiji to Australia (Melbourne, Tasmania, Sydney, and the area of Queensland).

Family Map Drill: Give each student a copy of an outline map of Australia. Encourage them to label all the states or territories that they know on the map. Compare their labeled states and territories with a labeled world map and make any necessary corrections. Then have them label one or two more states or territories on their maps, copying the spelling and location from the labeled world map.

Family Bible Study: Read together 1 Timothy 1, looking for any descriptions of promises, commands, sins, or principles. Record your findings in your *GOAL Bible Study Journal*. Older students should also be listening for doctrinal truths that they can add to their ongoing *Discovering Doctrine* books.

 Lesson 124: Napoleon the Conqueror

Materials Needed
• *Stories of the Nations, Volume 1*
• *The Year of the Horseless Carriage* (grades 7–12)
• *The Story of Modern France* (grades 7–9)
• *A Tale of Two Cities* (grades 10–12)

Family: Write "Napoleon" on a small whiteboard or sheet of paper. Explain that you are now going to read about a very famous man in history. Use the map on page 163 in *Stories of the Nations, Volume 1*, to find the locations mentioned in the chapter. Read together chapter 16, "Napoleon the Conqueror." Ask for an oral narration.

Grades 7–12: Read with your older children or assign as independent reading *The Year of the Horseless Carriage*, pages 11–24. Ask for an oral or written narration.

Grades 7–9: Also assign as independent reading *The Story of Modern France*, chapter 1, "The Old Monarchy." Ask for an oral or written narration.

Napoleon Bonaparte becomes Emperor of France (1804–1815)

Grades 10–12: Also assign as independent reading *A Tale of Two Cities,* Book 1, "Recalled to Life," chapters 1 and 2, "The Period" and "The Mail."

 # Lesson 125: Napoleon and the Grand Army

Materials Needed
- *Stories of the Nations, Volume 1*
- *The Year of the Horseless Carriage* (grades 7–12)
- *The Story of Modern France* (grades 7–9)
- *A Tale of Two Cities* (grades 10–12)

Family: Ask students what they recall from last time's reading about Napoleon. Read together *Stories of the Nations, Volume 1,* chapter 17, "Napoleon and the Grand Army." Use the map on page 163 to locate Moscow and see how far Napoleon's army had to march. Ask for an oral narration.

Grades 7–12: Read with your older children or assign as independent reading *The Year of the Horseless Carriage,* pages 25–42. Ask for an oral or written narration.

Grades 7–9: Also assign as independent reading *The Story of Modern France,* chapter 2, "The Minority of Louis XV." Ask for an oral or written narration.

Grades 10–12: Also assign as independent reading *A Tale of Two Cities,* Book 1, chapters 3 and 4, "The Night Shadows" and "The Preparation."

Tip: Make sure older children are up to date with their Book of Centuries entries.

Reminder: Get the book The Story of Napoleon *for grades 4–6 for lesson 135. Also get* Lafayette and the American Revolution *for grades 7–12.*

 # Lesson 126: Revolutionary Times, part 3

Materials Needed
- *Toliver's Secret* (grades 1–3)
- *A Young Patriot* (grades 4–6)
- *Early Thunder* OR *Johnny Tremain* (grades 7–9)
- *The Boys of '76* (grades 10–12)

Grades 1–3: Read together *Toliver's Secret,* chapter 11.

Book of Centuries
Timeline

Grades 4–6: Read with your older children or assign as independent reading *A Young Patriot,* the first half of chapter 3, "The Smell of Powder," pages 17–24. Ask for an oral or written narration.

Grades 7–9: Read with your older children or assign as independent reading *Early Thunder,* chapters 4 and 5, OR *Johnny Tremain,* chapter 3. Ask for an oral or written narration if desired.

Grades 10–12: Read with your older children or assign as independent reading *The Boys of '76,* chapter 25, "Affairs in Rhode Island." Ask for an oral or written narration.

 # Lesson 127: Revolutionary Times, part 4

Materials Needed
- *Toliver's Secret* (grades 1–3)
- *A Young Patriot* (grades 4–6)
- *Early Thunder* OR *Johnny Tremain* (grades 7–9)
- *The Boys of '76* (grades 10–12)

Grades 1–3: Read together *Toliver's Secret,* chapter 12.

Grades 4–6: Read with your older children or assign as independent reading *A Young Patriot,* the last half of chapter 3, "The Smell of Powder," pages 25–33. Ask for an oral or written narration.

Grades 7–9: Read with your older children or assign as independent reading *Early Thunder,* chapter 6, OR *Johnny Tremain,* chapter 4. Ask for an oral or written narration if desired.

Grades 10–12: Read with your older children or assign as independent reading *The Boys of '76,* chapter 26, "Affairs in South Carolina." Ask for an oral or written narration.

 # Lesson 128: Across the Indian Ocean & 1 Timothy 2 and 3

Materials Needed
- *Sailing Alone Around the World*
- Outline map of Australia; labeled world map
- Bible
- *GOAL Bible Study Journal*
- *Discovering Doctrine* (grades 7–12)

Family Geography Book: Ask students what they recall about Joshua Slocum's thoughts on Captain Cook. Read together *Sailing Alone Around*

Book of Centuries Timeline

the World, the last half of chapter 15, and ask for an oral narration. See if students can trace on the world map from Boston to Nova Scotia to the Azores to Gibraltar to Pernambuco to Rio de Janeiro to Uruguay to Buenos Aires to the Strait of Magellan to Juan Fernandez islands to the Marquesas islands to Samoa to Fiji to Australia (Melbourne, Tasmania, Sydney, and the area of Queensland) to Christmas Island.

Family Map Drill: Give each student a copy of an outline map of Australia. Encourage them to label all the states or territories that they know on the map. Compare their labeled states and territories with a labeled world map and make any necessary corrections. Then have them label one or two more states or territories on their maps, copying the spelling and location from the labeled world map.

Tip: The Australian parliament administers Christmas Island.

Reminder: Make sure you have outline maps of Central America for lesson 138.

Family Bible Study: Review your findings from last time and note how many of those items family members were able to put into practice during the week. Thank God for bringing His Word to your minds and giving you the strength to be doers, not just hearers. Read together 1 Timothy 2 and 3, looking for any descriptions of promises, commands, sins, or principles. Record your findings in your *GOAL Bible Study Journal*. Older students should also be listening for doctrinal truths that they can add to their ongoing *Discovering Doctrine* books.

Lesson 129: The Sailor and the Soldier

Materials Needed
- *Stories of the Nations, Volume 1*
- *The Year of the Horseless Carriage* (grades 7–12)
- *The Story of Modern France* (grades 7–9)
- *A Tale of Two Cities* (grades 10–12)

Family: Ask students what they recall from last time's reading about Napoleon and the Grand Army. Write "Nelson" and "Wellington" on a small whiteboard or sheet of paper. Explain that these were two Englishmen who fought significant battles against Napoleon. Read together *Stories of the Nations, Volume 1*, chapter 18, "The Sailor and the Soldier." Locate the battles mentioned on the map on page 163. Ask for an oral narration.

Grades 7–12: Read with your older children or assign as independent reading *The Year of the Horseless Carriage*, pages 43–57. Ask for an oral or written narration.

Grades 7–9: Also assign as independent reading *The Story of Modern*

France, chapter 3, "War of the Austrian Succession." Ask for an oral or written narration.

Grades 10–12: Also assign as independent reading *A Tale of Two Cities*, Book 1, chapters 5 and 6, "The Wine-Shop" and "The Shoemaker."

Reminder: Get the book Out of Darkness *for grades 1–3 for lesson 139.*

 # Lesson 130: Lafayette in Two Countries

Materials Needed
- *Stories of the Nations, Volume 1*
- *The Year of the Horseless Carriage* (grades 7–12)
- *The Story of Modern France* (grades 7–9)
- *A Tale of Two Cities* (grades 10–12)

Lafayette promotes liberty in U.S. and France (1757–1834)

Family: Ask students what they recall from last time's reading about Nelson and Wellington. Write "Lafayette" on a small whiteboard or sheet of paper. Explain that this is another Frenchman who lived at the time of Napoleon. Read together *Stories of the Nations, Volume 1*, chapter 19, "Lafayette in Two Countries." Ask for an oral narration.

Grades 7–12: Read with your older children or assign as independent reading *The Year of the Horseless Carriage*, pages 58–71. Ask for an oral or written narration.

Grades 7–9: Also assign as independent reading *The Story of Modern France*, chapter 4, "The Misgovernment of Louis XV." Ask for an oral or written narration.

Grades 10–12: Also assign as independent reading *A Tale of Two Cities*, Book 2, "The Golden Thread," chapters 1 and 2, "Five Years Later" and "A Sight."

Tip: Make sure older children are up to date with their Book of Centuries entries.

 # Lesson 131: Revolutionary Times, part 5

Materials Needed
- *Toliver's Secret* (grades 1–3)
- *A Young Patriot* (grades 4–6)
- *Early Thunder* OR *Johnny Tremain* (grades 7–9)
- *The Boys of '76* (grades 10–12)

Grades 1–3: Read together *Toliver's Secret*, chapter 13.

Grades 4–6: Read with your older children or assign as independent reading *A Young Patriot,* the first half of chapter 4, "Marching, Watching, Starving, and Freezing," pages 35–40. Ask for an oral or written narration.

Grades 7–9: Read with your older children or assign as independent reading *Early Thunder,* chapters 7 and 8, OR *Johnny Tremain,* chapter 5. Ask for an oral or written narration if desired.

Grades 10–12: Read with your older children or assign as independent reading *The Boys of '76,* chapter 27, "West Point." Ask for an oral or written narration.

Lesson 132: Valley Forge and Dark Days

Materials Needed
- *Stories of America, Volume 1*
- *A Young Patriot* (grades 4–6)
- *Early Thunder* OR *Johnny Tremain* (grades 7–9)
- *The Boys of '76* (grades 10–12)

Family: Ask students what they recall about George Washington and his troops' crossing the Delaware. Explain that Washington and his men endured many dark days during this war. Read together *Stories of America, Volume 1,* chapter 19, "Valley Forge and Dark Days." Ask for an oral narration.

Grades 4–6: Read with your older children or assign as independent reading *A Young Patriot,* the last half of chapter 4, "Marching, Watching, Starving, and Freezing," pages 41–47. Ask for an oral or written narration.

Grades 7–9: Read with your older children or assign as independent reading *Early Thunder,* chapter 9, OR *Johnny Tremain,* chapter 6. Ask for an oral or written narration if desired.

Grades 10–12: Read with your older children or assign as independent reading *The Boys of '76,* chapter 28, "King's Mountain and the Cowpens." Ask for an oral or written narration.

Lesson 133: Keeling Cocos Islands & 1 Timothy 4

Materials Needed
- *Sailing Alone Around the World*
- Outline map of Australia; labeled world map
- Bible

Book of Centuries Timeline

• *GOAL Bible Study Journal*
• *Discovering Doctrine* (grades 7–12)

Family Geography Book: Ask students what they recall about Joshua Slocum's voyage to Christmas Island. Read together *Sailing Alone Around the World*, the first half of chapter 16, and ask for an oral narration. See if students can trace on the world map from Boston to Nova Scotia to the Azores to Gibraltar to Pernambuco to Rio de Janeiro to Uruguay to Buenos Aires to the Strait of Magellan to Juan Fernandez islands to the Marquesas islands to Samoa to Fiji to Australia (Melbourne, Tasmania, Sydney, and the area of Queensland) to Christmas Island to the Cocos Islands.

Family Map Drill: Give each student a copy of an outline map of Australia. Encourage them to label all the states or territories that they know on the map. Compare their labeled states and territories with a labeled world map and make any necessary corrections. Then have them label one or two more states or territories on their maps, copying the spelling and location from the labeled world map.

Tip: The Australian parliament administers the Cocos Islands.

Family Bible Study: Review your findings from last time and note how many of those items family members were able to put into practice during the week. Thank God for bringing His Word to your minds and giving you the strength to be doers, not just hearers. Read together 1 Timothy 4, looking for any descriptions of promises, commands, sins, or principles. Record your findings in your *GOAL Bible Study Journal*. Older students should also be listening for doctrinal truths that they can add to their ongoing *Discovering Doctrine* books.

 # Lesson 134: Bolivar the Liberator

Materials Needed
• *Stories of the Nations, Volume 1*
• *The Year of the Horseless Carriage* (grades 7–12)
• *The Story of Modern France* (grades 7–9)
• *A Tale of Two Cities* (grades 10–12)

Family: Ask students what they recall from last time's reading about Lafayette. Write "Bolivar" on a small whiteboard or sheet of paper and ask if that name looks like any countries the students know. Explain that the time of Napoleon was a time of many revolutions across the world. Today's story will be about a man who helped win a revolution in South America. Read together *Stories of the Nations, Volume 1*, chapter 20, "Bolivar the Liberator." Have students locate the countries on the map on page 165 as they are mentioned in the chapter. Ask for an oral narration.

Grades 7–12: Read with your older children or assign as independent

Bolivar liberates Hispanic America (1783–1830)

reading *The Year of the Horseless Carriage,* pages 72–92. Ask for an oral or written narration.

Grades 7–9: Also assign as independent reading *The Story of Modern France,* chapter 5, "Marriage of Marie Antoinette." Ask for an oral or written narration.

Grades 10–12: Also assign as independent reading *A Tale of Two Cities,* Book 2, chapters 3 and 4, "A Disappointment" and "Congratulatory."

Book of Centuries Timeline

 # Lesson 135: Toussaint Fights for Haiti

Materials Needed
- *Stories of the Nations, Volume 1*
- *The Story of Napoleon* (grades 4–6)
- *Lafayette and the American Revolution* (grades 7–12)
- *The Story of Modern France* (grades 7–9)
- *A Tale of Two Cities* (grades 10–12)

Family: Ask students what they recall from last time's reading about Bolivar. Write "Toussaint L'Overture" on a small whiteboard or sheet of paper. Have students locate Haiti on the map on page 165 of *Stories of the Nations, Volume 1,* then read together chapter 21, "Toussaint Fights for Haiti." Ask for an oral narration.

Toussaint fights to liberate Haiti (1791–1803)

Grades 4–6: Read with your older children or assign as independent reading *The Story of Napoleon,* chapter 1, "Napoleon in School." Ask for an oral or written narration.

Grades 7–12: Read with your older children or assign as independent reading *Lafayette and the American Revolution,* chapter 1, "The Mysterious Stranger." Ask for an oral or written narration.

Grades 7–9: Also assign as independent reading *The Story of Modern France,* chapter 6, "Beginning of Louis XVI's Reign." Ask for an oral or written narration.

Grades 10–12: Also assign as independent reading *A Tale of Two Cities,* Book 2, chapters 5 and 6, "The Jackal" and "Hundreds of People."

Tip: Make sure older children are up to date with their Book of Centuries entries.

 # Lesson 136: John Paul Jones

Materials Needed
- *Stories of America, Volume 1*

• *A Young Patriot* (grades 4–6)
• *Early Thunder* OR *Johnny Tremain* (grades 7–9)
• *The Boys of '76* (grades 10–12)

Family: Ask the students what they recall from last time's reading about Valley Forge and Benedict Arnold. Explain that while Washington was battling on land, other Americans were fighting with British ships at sea. Read together *Stories of America, Volume 1*, chapter 20, "John Paul Jones, Naval Hero of the Revolution." Ask for an oral narration.

Grades 4–6: Read with your older children or assign as independent reading *A Young Patriot,* the first part of chapter 5, "Sending the Lobsterbacks Scurrying," pages 49–54. Ask for an oral or written narration.

Grades 7–9: Read with your older children or assign as independent reading *Early Thunder,* chapter 10, OR *Johnny Tremain,* chapter 7. Ask for an oral or written narration if desired.

Grades 10–12: Read with your older children or assign as independent reading *The Boys of '76,* chapter 29, "General Greene's Retreat." Ask for an oral or written narration.

Lesson 137: Marion, the Swamp Fox

Materials Needed
• *Stories of America, Volume 1*
• *A Young Patriot* (grades 4–6)
• *Early Thunder* OR *Johnny Tremain* (grades 7–9)
• *The Boys of '76* (grades 10–12)

Family: Ask the students what they recall from last time's reading about John Paul Jones. Explain that the Revolutionary War had many fronts. Washington fought in the North; John Paul Jones fought on the ocean; and other battles were taking place in the South. Write "Francis Marion" on a sheet of paper or whiteboard. Read together *Stories of America, Volume 1*, chapter 21, "Marion, the Swamp Fox." Ask for an oral narration.

Grades 4–6: Read with your older children or assign as independent reading *A Young Patriot,* the second part of chapter 5, "Sending the Lobsterbacks Scurrying," pages 55–61. Ask for an oral or written narration.

Grades 7–9: Read with your older children or assign as independent reading *Early Thunder,* chapter 11, OR *Johnny Tremain,* chapter 8. Ask for an oral or written narration if desired.

Grades 10–12: Read with your older children or assign as independent reading *The Boys of '76,* chapter 30. Ask for an oral or written narration.

Reminder: Get the book Benjamin Franklin *for grades 1–3 for lesson*

147. Also get Lewis and Clark: The Journey of the Corps of Discovery *for grades 7–12.*

Lesson 138: Away to Rodriguez & 1 Timothy 5

Materials Needed
- *Sailing Alone Around the World*
- Outline map of Central America; labeled world map
- Bible
- *GOAL Bible Study Journal*
- *Discovering Doctrine* (grades 7–12)

Family Geography Book: See if students can trace on the world map from Boston to Nova Scotia to the Azores to Gibraltar to Pernambuco to Rio de Janeiro to Uruguay to Buenos Aires to the Strait of Magellan to Juan Fernandez islands to the Marquesas islands to Samoa to Fiji to Australia (Melbourne, Tasmania, Sydney, and the area of Queensland) to Christmas Island to the Cocos Islands. Ask students what they recall about Joshua Slocum's voyage to the Cocos Islands. Read together *Sailing Alone Around the World*, the last half of chapter 16, and ask for an oral narration.

Family Map Drill: Give each student a copy of an outline map of Central America. Encourage them to label all the countries that they know on the map. Compare their labeled countries with a labeled world map and make any necessary corrections. Then have them label two or three more countries on their maps, copying the spelling and locations from the labeled world map.

Family Bible Study: Review your findings from last time then read together 1 Timothy 5, looking for any descriptions of promises, commands, sins, or principles. Record your findings in your *GOAL Bible Study Journal*. Older students should also be listening for doctrinal truths that they can add to their ongoing *Discovering Doctrine* books.

Lesson 139: Napoleonic Era, part 1

Materials Needed
- *Out of Darkness* (grades 1–3)
- *The Story of Napoleon* (grades 4–6)
- *Lafayette and the American Revolution* (grades 7–12)
- *The Story of Modern France* (grades 7–9)
- *A Tale of Two Cities* (grades 10–12)

Grades 1–3: Explain that Louis Braille lived during this time in history. Ask students what they may already know about Braille, and explain that you will read his story. Read together *Out of Darkness*, chapter 1, "The Dormitory."

Grades 4–6: Read with your older children or assign as independent reading *The Story of Napoleon*, chapter 2, "Napoleon an Officer." Ask for an oral or written narration.

Grades 7–12: Read with your older children or assign as independent reading *Lafayette and the American Revolution*, chapter 2, "The Little Lord of Chavaniac." Ask for an oral or written narration.

Grades 7–9: Also assign as independent reading *The Story of Modern France*, chapter 7, "Turgot's Ministry." Ask for an oral or written narration.

Grades 10–12: Also assign as independent reading *A Tale of Two Cities*, Book 2, chapters 7 and 8, "Monseigneur in Town" and "Monseigneur in the Country."

 # Lesson 140: Napoleonic Era, part 2

Materials Needed
- *Out of Darkness* (grades 1–3)
- *The Story of Napoleon* (grades 4–6)
- *Lafayette and the American Revolution* (grades 7–12)
- *The Story of Modern France* (grades 7–9)
- *A Tale of Two Cities* (grades 10–12)

Grades 1–3: Ask students what they recall from last time's reading about Louis Braille. Read together *Out of Darkness*, chapter 2, "The Accident."

Grades 4–6: Read with your older children or assign as independent reading *The Story of Napoleon*, chapter 3, "Napoleon in Egypt." Ask for an oral or written narration.

Grades 7–12: Read with your older children or assign as independent reading *Lafayette and the American Revolution*, chapter 3, "Why Not?" Ask for an oral or written narration.

Grades 7–9: Also assign as independent reading *The Story of Modern France*, chapter 8, "The American Revolution." Ask for an oral or written narration.

Grades 10–12: Also assign as independent reading *A Tale of Two Cities*, Book 2, chapters 9 and 10, "The Gorgon's Head" and "Two Promises."

Tip: Make sure older children are up to date with their Book of Centuries entries.

 # Lesson 141: General Greene

Materials Needed
- *Stories of America, Volume 1*

- *A Young Patriot* (grades 4–6)
- *Early Thunder* OR *Johnny Tremain* (grades 7–9)
- *The Boys of '76* (grades 10–12)

Family: Ask the students what they recall from last time's reading about Marion, the Swamp Fox. Explain that today's reading will be about another general in the American army who did much good for the American cause in the war. Read together *Stories of America, Volume 1*, chapter 22, "General Greene." Ask for an oral narration.

British surrender at Yorktown (1781)

Look at the map on page 183 to see what America looked like before the Revolutionary War and after it.

Grades 4–6: Read with your older children or assign as independent reading *A Young Patriot*, the last part of chapter 5, "Sending the Lobsterbacks Scurrying," pages 62–67. Ask for an oral or written narration.

Grades 7–9: Read with your older children or assign as independent reading *Early Thunder*, chapter 12, OR *Johnny Tremain*, chapter 9. Ask for an oral or written narration if desired.

Grades 10–12: Read with your older children or assign as independent reading *The Boys of '76*, chapter 31, "Eutaw." Ask for an oral or written narration.

Reminder: Get the book Amos Fortune, Free Man *for grades 4–6 for lesson 151.*

🇺🇸 Lesson 142: The Voyage of Our Ship of State

Materials Needed
- *Stories of America, Volume 1*
- *A Young Patriot* (grades 4–6)
- *Early Thunder* OR *Johnny Tremain* (grades 7–9)
- *The Boys of '76* (grades 10–12)
- *American Voices* (grades 10–12)

Family: Ask the students what they recall from last time's reading about General Greene and the end of the war. Explain that now that America was free, the people had to decide who would make the laws and who would enforce those laws. Read together *Stories of America, Volume 1*, chapter 23, "The Voyage of Our Ship of State." Ask for an oral narration.

U.S. Constitution written (1787)

Read together the poem "Sail On, O Ship of State" from *Stories of America, Volume 1*, page 143.

Grades 4–6: Read with your older children or assign as independent reading *A Young Patriot*, the first half of chapter 6, "The War and Joseph Go

South," pages 69–74. Ask for an oral or written narration.

Grades 7–9: Read with your older children or assign as independent reading *Early Thunder,* chapter 13, OR *Johnny Tremain*, chapter 10. Ask for an oral or written narration if desired.

Grades 10–12: Read with your older children or assign as independent reading *The Boys of '76,* chapter 32, "Fort Griswold." Ask for an oral or written narration.

Also read with your older children or assign as independent reading *American Voices,* pages 57–71, "Constitution of the United States," and ask for a narration. (If your student is planning to complete an American Government course that focuses on the Constitution, you may want to simply introduce the document at this time and save a thorough reading for that course.)

Lesson 143: A clean bill of health at Mauritius & 1 Timothy 6

Materials Needed
- *Sailing Alone Around the World*
- Outline map of Central America; labeled world map
- Bible
- *GOAL Bible Study Journal*
- *Discovering Doctrine* (grades 7–12)

Family Geography Book: Ask students what they recall about Joshua Slocum's time at the Cocos Island. Read together *Sailing Alone Around the World*, the first half of chapter 17, and ask for an oral narration. See if students can trace on the world map from Boston to Nova Scotia to the Azores to Gibraltar to Pernambuco to Rio de Janeiro to Uruguay to Buenos Aires to the Strait of Magellan to Juan Fernandez islands to the Marquesas islands to Samoa to Fiji to Australia (Melbourne, Tasmania, Sydney, and the area of Queensland) to Christmas Island to the Cocos Islands to Mauritius (east of Madagascar).

Family Map Drill: Give each student a copy of an outline map of Central America. Encourage them to label all the countries that they know on the map. Compare their labeled countries with a labeled world map and make any necessary corrections. Then have them label two or three more countries on their maps, copying the spelling and locations from the labeled world map.

Family Bible Study: Review your findings from last time then read together 1 Timothy 6, looking for any descriptions of promises, commands, sins, or principles. Record your findings in your *GOAL Bible Study Journal*. Older students should also be listening for doctrinal truths that they can add to their ongoing *Discovering Doctrine* books.

Lesson 144: Napoleonic Era, part 3

Materials Needed
- *Out of Darkness* (grades 1–3)
- *The Story of Napoleon* (grades 4–6)
- *Lafayette and the American Revolution* (grades 7–12)
- *The Story of Modern France* (grades 7–9)
- *A Tale of Two Cities* (grades 10–12)

Grades 1–3: Ask students what they recall from last time's reading about Louis Braille. Read together *Out of Darkness*, chapter 3, "The Little Blind Boy."

Grades 4–6: Read with your older children or assign as independent reading *The Story of Napoleon*, chapter 4, "Napoleon as Consul." Ask for an oral or written narration.

Grades 7–12: Read with your older children or assign as independent reading *Lafayette and the American Revolution*, chapter 4, "Escape from France." Ask for an oral or written narration.

Grades 7–9: Also assign as independent reading *The Story of Modern France*, chapter 9, "The Queen's Necklace." Ask for an oral or written narration.

Grades 10–12: Also assign as independent reading *A Tale of Two Cities*, Book 2, chapters 11 and 12, "A Companion Picture" and "The Fellow of Delicacy."

 # Lesson 145: Napoleonic Era, part 4

Materials Needed
- *Out of Darkness* (grades 1–3)
- *The Story of Napoleon* (grades 4–6)
- *Lafayette and the American Revolution* (grades 7–12)
- *The Story of Modern France* (grades 7–9)
- *A Tale of Two Cities* (grades 10–12)

Grades 1–3: Ask students what they recall from last time's reading about Louis Braille. Read together *Out of Darkness*, chapter 4, "The Royal Institute for Blind Youth."

Grades 4–6: Read with your older children or assign as independent reading *The Story of Napoleon*, chapter 5, "Napoleon as Emperor." Ask for an oral or written narration.

Grades 7–12: Read with your older children or assign as independent reading *Lafayette and the American Revolution*, chapter 5, "Here to Learn." Ask for an oral or written narration.

Grades 7–9: Also assign as independent reading *The Story of Modern France*, chapter 10, "The Fall of the Bastille." Ask for an oral or written narration.

Book of Centuries Timeline

George Washington elected first president of U.S. (1788)

Grades 10–12: Also assign as independent reading *A Tale of Two Cities*, Book 2, chapters 13 and 14, "The Fellow of No Delicacy" and "The Honest Tradesman."

Tip: Make sure older children are up to date with their Book of Centuries entries.

Lesson 146: President Washington

Materials Needed
- *Stories of America, Volume 1*
- *A Young Patriot* (grades 4–6)
- *Early Thunder* OR *Johnny Tremain* (grades 7–9)
- *The Boys of '76* (grades 10–12)
- *American Voices* (grades 10–12)

Family: Ask the students what they recall from last time's reading about America's new government. Explain that now that America had its new government figured out, it needed a President. Read together *Stories of America, Volume 1*, chapter 24, "President Washington." Ask for an oral narration.

Grades 4–6: Read with your older children or assign as independent reading *A Young Patriot*, the last half of chapter 6, "The War and Joseph Go South," pages 75–82. Ask for an oral or written narration.

Grades 7–9: Read with your older children or assign as independent reading *Early Thunder*, chapter 14, OR *Johnny Tremain*, chapters 11 and 12. Ask for an oral or written narration if desired.

Grades 10–12: Read with your older children or assign as independent reading *The Boys of '76*, chapter 33, "Yorktown," and the Conclusion. Ask for an oral or written narration.

Also assign as independent reading *American Voices*, pages 77–80, "George Washington's First Inaugural Address" and "George Washington's Thanksgiving Proclamation," and ask for a narration.

Lesson 147: The Young U. S. A., part 1

Materials Needed
- *Benjamin Franklin* (grades 1–3)
- *A Young Patriot* (grades 4–6)
- *Lewis and Clark: The Journey of the Corps of Discovery* (grades 7–12)
- *American Voices* (grades 10–12)

Grades 1–3: Ask the students what they might recall about Benjamin

Franklin from their readings so far. Have they heard anything about him? Read together *Benjamin Franklin*, pages 2–10. Ask for an oral narration.

Grades 4–6: Read with your older children or assign as independent reading *A Young Patriot,* chapters 7 and 8, "Parted Forever" and "A Cordial and Long Farewell." Ask for an oral or written narration.

Grades 7–12: Read with your older children or assign as independent reading *Lewis and Clark: The Journey of the Corps of Discovery*, chapter 1. Ask for an oral or written narration.

Grades 10–12: Also assign as independent reading *American Voices*, pages 81–90, "George Washington's Farewell Address," and ask for a narration.

> *Tip: Don't forget about the optional DVDs that correspond to the Lewis and Clark book. (See page 15 for details.) The cinematography is wonderful and will help make this study come alive. The set takes several hours to watch, so you will want to allow plenty of time to absorb it in segments over the next few weeks.*

Lesson 148: Leaving South Africa & Titus 1 and 2

Materials Needed
- *Sailing Alone Around the World*
- Outline map of Central America; labeled world map
- Bible
- *GOAL Bible Study Journal*
- *Discovering Doctrine* (grades 7–12)

Family Geography Book: See if students can trace on the world map from Boston to Nova Scotia to the Azores to Gibraltar to Pernambuco to Rio de Janeiro to Uruguay to Buenos Aires to the Strait of Magellan to Juan Fernandez islands to the Marquesas islands to Samoa to Fiji to Australia (Melbourne, Tasmania, Sydney, and the area of Queensland) to Christmas Island to the Cocos Islands to Mauritius. Ask students what they recall about Joshua Slocum's time in Mauritius. Read together *Sailing Alone Around the World*, the last half of chapter 17, and ask for an oral narration. Have students locate Durban in South Africa on the map.

> *Tip: You will read about the Boers later this term.*

Family Map Drill: Give each student a copy of an outline map of Central America. Encourage them to label all the countries that they know on the map. Compare their labeled countries with a labeled world map and make any necessary corrections. Then have them label two or three more countries on their maps, copying the spelling and locations from the labeled world map.

Family Bible Study: Review your findings from last time then read together Titus 1 and 2, looking for any descriptions of promises, commands, sins, or principles. Record your findings in your *GOAL Bible Study Journal.* Older students should also be listening for doctrinal truths that they can add to their ongoing *Discovering Doctrine* books.

 # Lesson 149: Napoleonic Era, part 5

Materials Needed
- *Out of Darkness* (grades 1–3)
- *The Story of Napoleon* (grades 4–6)
- *Lafayette and the American Revolution* (grades 7–12)
- *The Story of Modern France* (grades 7–9)
- *A Tale of Two Cities* (grades 10–12)

Grades 1–3: Ask students what they recall from last time's reading about Louis Braille. Read together *Out of Darkness,* chapter 5, "Nightwriting."

Grades 4–6: Read with your older children or assign as independent reading *The Story of Napoleon,* chapter 6, "Napoleon and Prussia." Ask for an oral or written narration.

Grades 7–12: Read with your older children or assign as independent reading *Lafayette and the American Revolution,* chapter 6, "Winter at Valley Forge." Ask for an oral or written narration.

Grades 7–9: Also assign as independent reading *The Story of Modern France,* chapter 11, "The Mob at Versailles." Ask for an oral or written narration.

Grades 10–12: Also assign as independent reading *A Tale of Two Cities,* Book 2, chapters 15 and 16, "Knitting" and "Still Knitting."

 # Lesson 150: Napoleonic Era, part 6

Materials Needed
- *Out of Darkness* (grades 1–3)
- *The Story of Napoleon* (grades 4–6)
- *Lafayette and the American Revolution* (grades 7–12)
- *The Story of Modern France* (grades 7–9)
- *A Tale of Two Cities* (grades 10–12)

Grades 1–3: Ask students what they recall from last time's reading about Louis Braille. Read together *Out of Darkness,* chapter 6, "The Braille Cell."

Grades 4–6: Read with your older children or assign as independent

reading *The Story of Napoleon,* chapter 7, "Napoleon in Spain." Ask for an oral or written narration.

Grades 7–12: Read with your older children or assign as independent reading *Lafayette and the American Revolution,* chapter 7, "The Battles of Barren Hill and Monmouth Courthouse." Ask for an oral or written narration.

Grades 7–9: Also assign as independent reading *The Story of Modern France,* chapter 12, "Death of Mirabeau." Ask for an oral or written narration.

Grades 10–12: Also assign as independent reading *A Tale of Two Cities,* Book 2, chapters 17 and 18, "One Night" and "Nine Days."

Tip: Make sure older children are up to date with their Book of Centuries entries.

 Lesson 151: The Young U. S. A., part 2

Materials Needed
- *Benjamin Franklin* (grades 1–3)
- *Amos Fortune, Free Man* (grades 4–6)
- *Lewis and Clark: The Journey of the Corps of Discovery* (grades 7–12)

Grades 1–3: Ask students what they remember from last time's reading about Benjamin Franklin's childhood. Read together *Benjamin Franklin,* pages 12–18. Ask for an oral narration.

Grades 4–6: Read with your older children or assign as independent reading *Amos Fortune, Free Man,* chapters 1 and 2. Ask for an oral or written narration.

Grades 7–12: Read with your older children or assign as independent reading *Lewis and Clark: The Journey of the Corps of Discovery,* chapter 2. Ask for an oral or written narration.

 Lesson 152: The Young U. S. A., part 3

Materials Needed
- *Benjamin Franklin* (grades 1–3)
- *Amos Fortune, Free Man* (grades 4–6)
- *Lewis and Clark: The Journey of the Corps of Discovery* (grades 7–12)

Grades 1–3: Ask students what they remember from last time's reading about Benjamin Franklin's trip to Philadelphia. Read together *Benjamin Franklin,* pages 20–28. Ask for an oral narration.

Grades 4–6: Read with your older children or assign as independent

reading *Amos Fortune, Free Man*, chapters 3 and 4. Ask for an oral or written narration.

Grades 7–12: Read with your older children or assign as independent reading *Lewis and Clark: The Journey of the Corps of Discovery*, chapter 3. Ask for an oral or written narration.

Lesson 153: Rounding the Cape of Storms & Titus 3

Materials Needed
- *Sailing Alone Around the World*
- Outline map of Central America; labeled world map
- Bible
- *GOAL Bible Study Journal*
- *Discovering Doctrine* (grades 7–12)

Family Geography Book: Ask students what they recall about Joshua Slocum's voyage to Durban and his time there. See if students can trace on the world map from Boston to Nova Scotia to the Azores to Gibraltar to Pernambuco to Rio de Janeiro to Uruguay to Buenos Aires to the Strait of Magellan to Juan Fernandez islands to the Marquesas islands to Samoa to Fiji to Australia (Melbourne, Tasmania, Sydney, and the area of Queensland) to Christmas Island to the Cocos Islands to Mauritius to Durban. Read together *Sailing Alone Around the World*, the first half of chapter 18, and ask for an oral narration.

Family Map Drill: Give each student a copy of an outline map of Central America. Encourage them to label all the countries that they know on the map. Compare their labeled countries with a labeled world map and make any necessary corrections. Then have them label two or three more countries on their maps, copying the spelling and locations from the labeled world map.

Family Bible Study: Review your findings from last time then read together Titus 3, looking for any descriptions of promises, commands, sins, or principles. Record your findings in your *GOAL Bible Study Journal*. Older students should also be listening for doctrinal truths that they can add to their ongoing *Discovering Doctrine* books.

Lesson 154: Napoleonic Era, part 7

Materials Needed
- *Out of Darkness* (grades 1–3)
- *The Story of Napoleon* (grades 4–6)

• *Lafayette and the American Revolution* (grades 7–12)
• *The Story of Modern France* (grades 7–9)
• *A Tale of Two Cities* (grades 10–12)

Grades 1–3: Ask students what they recall from last time's reading about Louis Braille. Read together *Out of Darkness,* chapter 7, "The Teacher."

Grades 4–6: Read with your older children or assign as independent reading *The Story of Napoleon,* chapter 8, "Napoleon in Russia." Ask for an oral or written narration.

Grades 7–12: Read with your older children or assign as independent reading *Lafayette and the American Revolution,* chapter 8, "Hero of Two Worlds." Ask for an oral or written narration.

Grades 7–9: Also assign as independent reading *The Story of Modern France,* chapter 13, "The Flight to Varennes." Ask for an oral or written narration.

Grades 10–12: Also assign as independent reading *A Tale of Two Cities,* Book 2, chapters 19 and 20, "An Opinion" and "A Plea."

 # Lesson 155: Napoleonic Era, part 8

Materials Needed
• *Out of Darkness* (grades 1–3)
• *The Story of Napoleon* (grades 4–6)
• *Lafayette and the American Revolution* (grades 7–12)
• *The Story of Modern France* (grades 7–9)
• *A Tale of Two Cities* (grades 10–12)

Grades 1–3: Ask students what they recall from last time's reading about Louis Braille. Read together *Out of Darkness,* chapter 8, "The Gift."

Grades 4–6: Read with your older children or assign as independent reading *The Story of Napoleon,* chapter 9, "Napoleon Emperor of Elba." Ask for an oral or written narration.

Grades 7–12: Read with your older children or assign as independent reading *Lafayette and the American Revolution,* chapter 9, "The Boy Cannot Escape Me." Ask for an oral or written narration.

Grades 7–9: Also assign as independent reading *The Story of Modern France,* chapter 14, "Mobs Raid the Tuileries." Ask for an oral or written narration.

Grades 10–12: Also assign as independent reading *A Tale of Two Cities,* Book 2, chapters 21 and 22, "Echoing Footsteps" and "The Sea Still Rises."

Tip: Make sure older children are up to date with their Book of Centuries entries.

Lesson 156: The Young U. S. A., part 4

Materials Needed
- *Benjamin Franklin* (grades 1–3)
- *Amos Fortune, Free Man* (grades 4–6)
- *Lewis and Clark: The Journey of the Corps of Discovery* (grades 7–12)
- *American Voices* (grades 10–12)

Grades 1–3: Ask students what they remember from last time's reading about Benjamin Franklin as a printer. Read together *Benjamin Franklin*, pages 30–38. Ask for an oral narration.

Grades 4–6: Read with your older children or assign as independent reading *Amos Fortune, Free Man,* chapters 5 and 6. Ask for an oral or written narration.

Grades 7–12: Read with your older children or assign as independent reading *Lewis and Clark: The Journey of the Corps of Discovery,* chapter 4. Ask for an oral or written narration.

Grades 10–12: Also assign as independent reading *American Voices,* page 94, "I Love Thy Kingdom, Lord."

 # Lesson 157: The Young U. S. A., part 5

Materials Needed
- *Benjamin Franklin* (grades 1–3)
- *Amos Fortune, Free Man* (grades 4–6)
- *Lewis and Clark: The Journey of the Corps of Discovery* (grades 7–12)
- *American Voices* (grades 10–12)

Grades 1–3: Ask students what they remember from last time's reading about Benjamin Franklin as an inventor. Read together *Benjamin Franklin*, pages 40–48. Ask for an oral narration.

Grades 4–6: Read with your older children or assign as independent reading *Amos Fortune, Free Man,* chapters 7 and 8. Ask for an oral or written narration.

Grades 7–12: Read with your older children or assign as independent reading *Lewis and Clark: The Journey of the Corps of Discovery,* chapter 5. Ask for an oral or written narration.

Grades 10–12: Also assign as independent reading *American Voices,* pages 95–97, "Thomas Jefferson's First Inaugural Address," and ask for a narration.

 # Lesson 158: Off for St. Helena & 2 Timothy 1

Materials Needed
- *Sailing Alone Around the World*

- Outline map of Central America; labeled world map
- Bible
- *GOAL Bible Study Journal*
- *Discovering Doctrine* (grades 7–12)

Family Geography Book: Ask students what they recall about Joshua Slocum's time in Cape Town. See if students can trace on the world map from Boston to Nova Scotia to the Azores to Gibraltar to Pernambuco to Rio de Janeiro to Uruguay to Buenos Aires to the Strait of Magellan to Juan Fernandez islands to the Marquesas islands to Samoa to Fiji to Australia (Melbourne, Tasmania, Sydney, and the area of Queensland) to Christmas Island to the Cocos Islands to Mauritius to Durban to Cape Town. Read together *Sailing Alone Around the World*, the last half of chapter 18, and ask for an oral narration.

Family Map Drill: Give each student a copy of an outline map of Central America. Encourage them to label all the countries that they know on the map. Compare their labeled countries with a labeled world map and make any necessary corrections. Then have them label two or three more countries on their maps, copying the spelling and locations from the labeled world map.

Family Bible Study: Review your findings from last time then read together 2 Timothy 1, looking for any descriptions of promises, commands, sins, or principles. Record your findings in your *GOAL Bible Study Journal*. Older students should also be listening for doctrinal truths that they can add to their ongoing *Discovering Doctrine* books.

Lesson 159: The Boers Settle in Africa

Materials Needed
- *Stories of the Nations, Volume 1*
- *The Story of Napoleon* (grades 4–6)
- *Lafayette and the American Revolution* (grades 7–12)
- *The Story of Modern France* (grades 7–9)
- *A Tale of Two Cities* (grades 10–12)

Family: Write "Boers" in a small whiteboard or sheet of paper. Explain that this group of people are connected with the history of Africa. Read together *Stories of the Nations, Volume 1*, chapter 22, "The Boers Settle in Africa." Use the map on page 165 to locate the places mentioned in the chapter. Ask for an oral narration.

Boers establish Orange River Free State and Transvaal Republic in Africa (1840)

Tip: You might see if the students recall hearing about Boers in Joshua Slocum's travels.

Grades 4–6: Read with your older children or assign as independent

reading *The Story of Napoleon*, chapter 10, "Napoleon's Last Battle." Ask for an oral or written narration.

Grades 7–12: Read with your older children or assign as independent reading *Lafayette and the American Revolution*, chapter 10, "In Search of Liberty." Ask for an oral or written narration.

Grades 7–9: Also assign as independent reading *The Story of Modern France*, chapter 15, "The King's Trial." Ask for an oral or written narration.

Grades 10–12: Also assign as independent reading *A Tale of Two Cities*, Book 2, chapters 23 and 24, "Fire Rises" and "Drawn to the Loadstone Rock."

 Lesson 160: How Samuel Morse Connected the Nations

Materials Needed
- *Stories of the Nations, Volume 1*
- *Hearts and Hands* (grades 7–12)
- *The Story of Modern France* (grades 7–9)
- *A Tale of Two Cities* (grades 10–12)

Family: Ask students what they recall from last time's reading about the Boers in Africa. Write "Samuel Morse" on a small whiteboard or sheet of paper. Read together *Stories of the Nations, Volume 1*, chapter 23, "How Samuel Morse Connected the Nations." Ask for an oral narration.

Samuel Morse invents the telegraph (1837)

Grades 7–12: Read with your older children or assign as independent reading *Hearts and Hands*, "Revolutions and Rebellions" and "Liang Fa." Ask for an oral or written narration.

Grades 7–9: Also assign as independent reading *The Story of Modern France*, chapter 16, "The King's Execution." Ask for an oral or written narration.

Grades 10–12: Also assign as independent reading *A Tale of Two Cities*, Book 3, "The Track of a Storm," chapters 1 and 2, "In Secret" and "The Grindstone."

Tip: Make sure older children are up to date with their Book of Centuries entries.

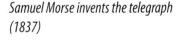 **Lesson 161: America Grows**

Materials Needed
- *Stories of America, Volume 1*
- *Amos Fortune, Free Man* (grades 4–6)
- *Lewis and Clark: The Journey of the Corps of Discovery* (grades 7–12)
- *American Voices* (grades 10–12)

Family: Ask students what they remember about George Washington as President. Read together *Stories of America, Volume 1*, chapter 25, "America Grows." Ask for an oral narration. Use the map on page 185 to show what land was added in the Louisiana Purchase and how it related to other countries' territories.

Grades 4–6: Read with your older children or assign as independent reading *Amos Fortune, Free Man*, chapters 9 and 10. Ask for an oral or written narration.

Grades 7–12: Read with your older children or assign as independent reading *Lewis and Clark: The Journey of the Corps of Discovery*, chapter 6. Ask for an oral or written narration.

Grades 10–12: Also assign as independent reading *American Voices*, pages 103–106, "Letters from John Adams and Thomas Jefferson (excerpts)," and ask for a narration.

Book of Centuries Timeline

Lewis and Clark explore the Louisiana Purchase (1804–1806)

Lesson 162: The Steamboat and the Cotton Gin

Materials Needed
- *Stories of America, Volume 1*
- *Amos Fortune, Free Man* (grades 4–6)
- *Lewis and Clark: The Journey of the Corps of Discovery* (grades 7–12)

Family: Ask students what they recall about Lewis and Clark and the growth of America. Read together *Stories of America, Volume 1*, chapter 26, "The Steamboat and the Cotton Gin." Ask for an oral narration.

Grades 4–6: Read with your older children or assign as independent reading *Amos Fortune, Free Man*, chapters 11 and 12. Ask for an oral or written narration.

Grades 7–12: Read with your older children or assign as independent reading *Lewis and Clark: The Journey of the Corps of Discovery*, chapter 7. Ask for an oral or written narration.

Fulton's steamboat (1807)

Eli Whitney invents the cotton gin (1795)

Lesson 163: In the isle of Napoleon's exile & 2 Timothy 2

Materials Needed
- *Sailing Alone Around the World*
- Outline map of Central America; labeled world map
- Bible

Book of Centuries Timeline

• *GOAL Bible Study Journal*
• *Discovering Doctrine* (grades 7–12)

Family Geography Book: See if students can trace on the world map from Boston to Nova Scotia to the Azores to Gibraltar to Pernambuco to Rio de Janeiro to Uruguay to Buenos Aires to the Strait of Magellan to Juan Fernandez islands to the Marquesas islands to Samoa to Fiji to Australia (Melbourne, Tasmania, Sydney, and the area of Queensland) to Christmas Island to the Cocos Islands to Mauritius to Durban to Cape Town to St. Helena. Ask students what they recall about Joshua Slocum's sailing for St. Helena. Read together *Sailing Alone Around the World*, chapter 19, and ask for an oral narration.

Family Map Drill: Give each student a copy of an outline map of Central America. Encourage them to label all the countries that they know on the map. Compare their labeled countries with a labeled world map and make any necessary corrections. Then have them label two or three more countries on their maps, copying the spelling and locations from the labeled world map.

Family Bible Study: Review your findings from last time then read together 2 Timothy 2, looking for any descriptions of promises, commands, sins, or principles. Record your findings in your *GOAL Bible Study Journal*. Older students should also be listening for doctrinal truths that they can add to their ongoing *Discovering Doctrine* books.

Lesson 164: When Russia Fought the Turks Again

Materials Needed
• *Stories of the Nations, Volume 1*
• *Hearts and Hands* (grades 7–12)
• *The Story of Modern France* (grades 7–9)
• *A Tale of Two Cities* (grades 10–12)

Crimean War (1854–1856)

Family: Ask students what they recall from last time's reading about Samuel Morse. Write "Crimea" on a small whiteboard or sheet of paper and have students find it on the map on page 157 of *Stories of the Nations, Volume 1*. Read together chapter 24, "When Russia Fought the Turks Again." Ask for an oral narration.

Grades 7–12: Read with your older children or assign as independent reading *Hearts and Hands,* "A New Method of Missions" and "Adoniram and Ann Judson." Ask for an oral or written narration.

Grades 7–9: Also assign as independent reading *The Story of Modern France*, chapter 17, "Story of Charlotte Corday." Ask for an oral or written narration.

Grades 10–12: Also assign as independent reading *A Tale of Two Cities,* Book 3, chapters 3 and 4, "The Shadow" and "Calm in Storm."

 # Lesson 165: Commodore Perry Opens the Door to Japan

Materials Needed
- *Stories of the Nations, Volume 1*
- *Hearts and Hands* (grades 7–12)
- *The Story of Modern France* (grades 7–9)
- *A Tale of Two Cities* (grades 10–12)

Family: Ask students what they recall from last time's reading about the Crimean War. Read together *Stories of the Nations, Volume 1,* chapter 25, "Commodore Perry Opens the Door to Japan." Have students find Japan on the map on page 165 as it is mentioned in the chapter. Ask for an oral narration.

Grades 7–12: Read with your older children or assign as independent reading *Hearts and Hands,* "Fidelia Fiske." Ask for an oral or written narration.

Grades 7–9: Also assign as independent reading *The Story of Modern France,* chapter 18, "The Queen Parted from Her Children." Ask for an oral or written narration.

Grades 10–12: Also assign as independent reading *A Tale of Two Cities,* Book 3, chapters 5 and 6, "The Wood-Sawyer" and "Triumph."

Tip: Make sure older children are up to date with their Book of Centuries entries.

 # Lesson 166: Song about Thanksgiving Day

Materials Needed
- *Stories of America, Volume 1*
- *Amos Fortune, Free Man* (grades 4–6)
- *Lewis and Clark: The Journey of the Corps of Discovery* (grades 7–12)

Family: Ask students what they recall about the inventions of the steamboat and the cotton gin. Explain that today's reading will be a poem that gives us a picture of life during the early 1800s. Read the title of the poem first and see if any of the students recall how Thanksgiving Day was started in America. Read together the poem "The New-England Boy's Song

Book of Centuries Timeline

Perry negotiates U.S. trade treaty with Japan (1854)

about Thanksgiving Day" from *Stories of America, Volume 1,* pages 161 and 162.

Grades 4–6: Read with your older children or assign as independent reading *Amos Fortune, Free Man,* chapters 13 and 14. Ask for an oral or written narration.

Grades 7–12: Read with your older children or assign as independent reading *Lewis and Clark: The Journey of the Corps of Discovery,* chapter 8. Ask for an oral or written narration.

Lesson 167: War of 1812

Materials Needed
- *Stories of America, Volume 1*
- *Amos Fortune, Free Man* (grades 4–6)
- *Lewis and Clark: The Journey of the Corps of Discovery* (grades 7–12)
- *American Voices* (grades 10–12)

War of 1812 between England and U.S. (1812–1815)

Family: Read together *Stories of America, Volume 1,* chapter 27, "How the English and the Americans Fought Again." Ask for an oral narration.

Grades 4–6: Read with your older children or assign as independent reading *Amos Fortune, Free Man,* chapters 15 and 16. Ask for an oral or written narration.

Grades 7–12: Read with your older children or assign as independent reading *Lewis and Clark: The Journey of the Corps of Discovery,* chapter 9. Ask for an oral or written narration.

Grades 10–12: Also assign as independent reading *American Voices,* pages 108–110, "Poems by William Cullen Bryant."

Lesson 168: Off Cape St. Roque, Brazil & 2 Timothy 3

Materials Needed
- *Sailing Alone Around the World*
- Outline map of Central America; labeled world map
- Bible
- *GOAL Bible Study Journal*
- *Discovering Doctrine* (grades 7–12)

Family Geography Book: Ask students what they recall about Joshua Slocum's time on St. Helena. See if students can trace on the world map from Boston to Nova Scotia to the Azores to Gibraltar to Pernambuco to Rio de Janeiro to Uruguay to Buenos Aires to the Strait of Magellan to Juan

Fernandez islands to the Marquesas islands to Samoa to Fiji to Australia (Melbourne, Tasmania, Sydney, and the area of Queensland) to Christmas Island to the Cocos Islands to Mauritius to Durban to Cape Town to St. Helena to Ascension Island. Read together *Sailing Alone Around the World*, chapter 20, and ask for an oral narration.

Family Map Drill: Give each student a copy of an outline map of Central America. Encourage them to label all the countries that they know on the map. Compare their labeled countries with a labeled world map and make any necessary corrections. Then have them label two or three more countries on their maps, copying the spelling and locations from the labeled world map.

Family Bible Study: Review your findings from last time then read together 2 Timothy 3, looking for any descriptions of promises, commands, sins, or principles. Record your findings in your *GOAL Bible Study Journal*. Older students should also be listening for doctrinal truths that they can add to their ongoing *Discovering Doctrine* books.

 # Lesson 169: Another Napoleon

Materials Needed
- *Stories of the Nations, Volume 1*
- *Hearts and Hands* (grades 7–12)
- *The Story of Modern France* (grades 7–9)
- *A Tale of Two Cities* (grades 10–12)

Louis Napoleon rules France (1848–1852)

Family: Ask students what they recall from last time's reading about Commodore Perry and Japan. Explain that this time you will read about another Napoleon. Ask students what they think this Napoleon will be like. Read together *Stories of the Nations, Volume 1*, chapter 26, "Another Napoleon." Ask for an oral narration.

Grades 7–12: Read with your older children or assign as independent reading *Hearts and Hands,* "The Rise of Protestant Denominations" and "Sojourner Truth and Harriet Beecher Stowe." Ask for an oral or written narration.

Grades 7–9: Also assign as independent reading *The Story of Modern France*, chapter 19, "Death of Marie Antoinette." Ask for an oral or written narration.

Grades 10–12: Also assign as independent reading *A Tale of Two Cities*, Book 3, chapters 7 and 8, "A Knock at the Door" and "A Hand at Cards."

Lesson 170: Livingstone and Stanley Explore Africa

Materials Needed
- *Stories of the Nations, Volume 1*
- *Hearts and Hands* (grades 7–12)

Book of Centuries
Timeline

Livingstone and Stanley explore Africa (1849–1874)

• *The Story of Modern France* (grades 7–9)
• *A Tale of Two Cities* (grades 10–12)

Family: Ask students what they recall from last time's reading about Louis Napoleon. Write "Livingstone" on a small whiteboard or sheet of paper. Read together *Stories of the Nations, Volume 1*, chapter 27, "Livingstone and Stanley Explore Africa." Ask for an oral narration.

Grades 7–12: Read with your older children or assign as independent reading *Hearts and Hands*, "David Livingstone." Ask for an oral or written narration.

Grades 7–9: Also assign as independent reading *The Story of Modern France*, chapter 20, "Many Executions." Ask for an oral or written narration.

Grades 10–12: Also assign as independent reading *A Tale of Two Cities*, Book 3, chapters 9 and 10, "The Game Made" and "The Substance of the Shadow."

 # Lesson 171: Our National Anthem

Materials Needed
• *Stories of America, Volume 1*
• *Amos Fortune, Free Man* (grades 4–6)
• *Lewis and Clark: The Journey of the Corps of Discovery* (grades 7–12)
• *American Voices* (grades 10–12)

Family: Ask students what they recall from last time's reading about the War of 1812. Explain that a very important poem was written during one of the battles of that war. Read together *Stories of America, Volume 1*, chapter 28, "Our National Anthem." Ask for an oral narration.

Francis Scott Key writes The Star-Spangled Banner (1814)

Grades 4–6: Read with your older children or assign as independent reading *Amos Fortune, Free Man*, chapters 17 and 18. Ask for an oral or written narration.

Star-Spangled Banner adopted as U.S. National anthem (1931)

Grades 7–12: Read with your older children or assign as independent reading *Lewis and Clark: The Journey of the Corps of Discovery*, chapter 10. Ask for an oral or written narration.

Grades 10–12: Also assign as independent reading *American Voices*, pages 128–130, "My Faith Looks Up to Thee" and "Poems by Oliver Wendell Holmes Sr."

Reminder: If you want to do the optional hands-on project for lesson 177, start collecting the materials you will need.

 # Lesson 172: Remember the Alamo

Materials Needed
• *Stories of America, Volume 1*

*Book of Centuries
Timeline*

• *Amos Fortune, Free Man* (grades 4–6)
• *Lewis and Clark: The Journey of the Corps of Discovery* (grades 7–12)
• *American Voices* (grades 10–12)

Family: Ask students what they recall from last time's reading about the Star-Spangled Banner. Look in *Stories of America, Volume 1*, at the map on page 185 again and locate the Texas Annexation territory. Explain that it used to be ruled by Mexico. Write "Alamo" on a sheet of paper or whiteboard. Read together chapter 29, "Remember the Alamo." Ask for an oral narration.

Grades 4–6: Read with your older children or assign as independent reading *Amos Fortune, Free Man,* chapters 19 and 20. Ask for an oral or written narration.

Grades 7–12: Read with your older children or assign as independent reading *Lewis and Clark: The Journey of the Corps of Discovery*, chapter 11. Ask for an oral or written narration. (Note: Students will finish the book along with term exams next week.)

Grades 10–12: Also assign as independent reading *American Voices,* pages 134–136, "Democracy in America (excerpts)," and ask for a narration.

Mexicans attack the Americans in Texas at the Alamo (1836)

Mexican War (1846–1848)

Lesson 173: Clearing for home & 2 Timothy 4

Materials Needed
• *Sailing Alone Around the World*
• Outline map of Central America; labeled world map
• Bible
• *GOAL Bible Study Journal*
• *Discovering Doctrine* (grades 7–12)

Family Geography Book: Ask students what they recall about Joshua Slocum's voyage to Grenada. See if students can trace on the world map from Boston to Nova Scotia to the Azores to Gibraltar to Pernambuco to Rio de Janeiro to Uruguay to Buenos Aires to the Strait of Magellan to Juan Fernandez islands to the Marquesas islands to Samoa to Fiji to Australia (Melbourne, Tasmania, Sydney, and the area of Queensland) to Christmas Island to the Cocos Islands to Mauritius to Durban to Cape Town to St. Helena to Ascension Island to Grenada. Read together *Sailing Alone Around the World*, chapter 21, and ask for an oral narration. Trace Slocum's final leg of the journey back to Newport, Rhode Island, and finally, Fairhaven, Massachusetts.

Family Map Drill: Give each student a copy of an outline map of Central America. Encourage them to label all the countries that they know on the map. Compare their labeled countries with a labeled world map and make any necessary corrections. Then have them label two or three more countries on their maps, copying the spelling and locations from the labeled world map.

Family Bible Study: Review your findings from last time then read together 2 Timothy 4, looking for any descriptions of promises, commands, sins, or principles. Record your findings in your *GOAL Bible Study Journal*. Older students should also be listening for doctrinal truths that they can add to their ongoing *Discovering Doctrine* books.

 Lesson 174: Garibaldi, Hero of Italy

Materials Needed
- *Stories of the Nations, Volume 1*
- *Hearts and Hands* (grades 7–12)
- *The Story of Modern France* (grades 7–9)
- *A Tale of Two Cities* (grades 10–12)

Family: Ask students what they recall from last time's reading about Livingstone and Stanley. Write "Garibaldi" on a small whiteboard or sheet of paper and have students locate Italy on the map on page 163 of *Stories of the Nations, Volume 1*. Read together chapter 28, "Garibaldi, Hero of Italy." Ask for an oral narration.

Grades 7–12: Read with your older children or assign as independent reading *Hearts and Hands,* "Other Christians of the Awakening Church" and "The Beginnings of a Modern World." Ask for an oral or written narration.

Grades 7–9: Also assign as independent reading *The Story of Modern France,* chapter 21, "Death of Madam Elizabeth." Ask for an oral or written narration.

Grades 10–12: Also assign as independent reading *A Tale of Two Cities,* Book 3, chapters 11 and 12, "Dusk" and "Darkness."

 Lesson 175: World History Catch Up

Materials Needed
- *Stories of the Nations, Volume 1* (if needed for catching up)
- *The Story of Modern France* (grades 7–9)
- *A Tale of Two Cities* (grades 10–12)

Family: Use today to catch up on any assigned reading and narrations from *Stories of the Nations, Volume 1*.

Grades 7–9: Assign as independent reading *The Story of Modern France,* chapters 22 and 23, "Death of Robespierre" and "End of the Revolution." Ask for an oral or written narration.

Garibaldi unites Italy (1859–1861)

Tip: Students in grades 7–9 may read the rest of The Story of Modern France *in their leisure time if desired.*

Grades 10–12: Assign as independent reading *A Tale of Two Cities,* Book 3, chapters 13–15, "Fifty-Two," "The Knitting Done," and "The Footsteps Die Out For Ever."

Tip: Make sure older children are up to date with their Book of Centuries entries.

 ## Lesson 176: American History Exam

Materials Needed
- *Lewis and Clark: The Journey of the Corps of Discovery* (grades 7–12)

Family: Use the questions below to begin the students' exam on Early American history.

Tip: Exams in a Charlotte Mason school require no "cramming" or preparation. You may be pleasantly surprised at what your students remember with no prompting.

Grades 1–3: Tell about a time when America fought against England.
Grades 4–6: Tell the story of our National Anthem.
Grades 7–9: Describe the three branches of American government and what each is responsible to do.
Grades 10–12: Describe how America grew after the Revolutionary War, both in size and in greatness. Include her government, her territories, and her inventions.

Tip: You may want to assign the older students to write their exam answers. Younger students may do oral exams; you might want to write or type their answers as they tell what they know. Or, if you have students in more than one grade level, you might allow them to do their exams orally in a group. That way the older can hear the younger, and the younger can hear the older.

Grades 7–12: Read with your older children or assign as independent reading *Lewis and Clark: The Journey of the Corps of Discovery*, chapter 12. Ask for an oral or written narration.

 ## Lesson 177: American History Project or Exam

Materials Needed
- (optional) Materials for hands-on project

Family: Do a hands-on project (see below), or use the questions below to continue the students' exam on Early American history.

Grades 1–3: Tell about Benjamin Franklin.
Grades 4–6: Tell the story of Amos Fortune.
Grades 7–9: "We have met the enemy and they are ours." Who said this? Tell the story.
Grades 10–12: Tell in full about the War of 1812. Explain the causes of the war, some of the battles, and any benefits that came from it.

Optional Hands-On Project: Select a hands-on project from the Links and Tips page: http://SimplyCharlotteMason.com/books/early-modern/links-tips/

Lesson 178: Geography Exam & Bible Exam

Materials Needed
- Outline maps of South America, Australia, Central America
- (optional) Labeled world map

Geography Exam: Give each student an outline map of South America, Australia, and Central America. See how many countries/states or territories they can label.

Optional Additional Geography Exam: Give each student a labeled world map and see how many of the places listed below he can point out. All are places that Joshua Slocum visited on his trip around the world, but they are not listed in the order in which he visited them: Strait of Magellan, Cape Town, Rio de Janeiro, Australia (Melbourne, Tasmania, Sydney, and the area of Queensland), Nova Scotia, Buenos Aires, Samoa, Uruguay, Christmas Island, Fiji, St. Helena, Grenada.

Bible Exam: Use the questions below for the students' exam on Timothy and Titus.

Grades 1–3: Name two GOAL items you have found in 1 and 2 Timothy or Titus and been able to do, not just hear.
Grades 4–12: Name the four things you are looking for in the Bible passages you have been reading (GOAL) and give at least one example of each from 1 Timothy, Titus, or 2 Timothy.

Tip: If you assigned Scripture memory from 1 Timothy, Titus, or 2 Timothy, you might also ask for a recitation of the passage(s). Be sure to encourage the children to say beautiful words in a beautiful way as they recite.

Lesson 179: World History Exam

Family: Use the questions below to continue the students' exam on Early Modern world history.

Grades 1–3: Tell a story from your reading of a man who fought in a battle.
Grades 4–6: What is a revolution? Tell the story of one of these men who fought in a revolution: Lafayette, Bolivar, Touissant, Garibaldi.
Grades 7–9: Select three liberators and tell their stories: Lafayette, Bolivar, Touissant, Garibaldi.
Grades 10–12: "Lafayette, we are here." Explain fully why that U.S. Colonel's statement summarized French-American friendship.

Lesson 180: World History Exam

Family: Use the questions below to finish the students' exam on Early Modern world history.

Grades 1–3: Tell a story from your reading of a man who invented or discovered something.
Grades 4–6: Tell all you remember about Napoleon.
Grades 7–9: Tell fully about the French Revolution.
Grades 10–12: This age in history is sometimes called the Age of Revolution. Explain why that might be a good name, giving the stories of at least three examples from your reading. Explain what each was revolting against and what the results of the revolutions were.